Methuen C17 4/53 12/83
850

AN ASSESSMENT OF
TWENTIETH-CENTURY LITERATURE

AN ASSESSMENT OF TWENTIETH-CENTURY LITERATURE

Six Lectures
Delivered in the
B.B.C. Third Programme

BY

J. ISAACS

LONDON
SECKER & WARBURG
1952

MARTIN SECKER & WARBURG LTD.,
7 John Street, Bloomsbury,
London, W.C.1

First published 1951
Reprinted 1952

Printed and bound in Great Britain by
The Camelot Press Ltd., London and Southampton

Contents

Preface

THESE lectures, which were delivered in the Third Programme of the B.B.C. in September and October, 1950, are here printed as spoken, with the restoration of some passages omitted for lack of time. The peculiarities of style and emphasis, the deliberately bad or rhetorical grammar necessitated by a spoken style, have been retained. The conditioned listener will recognise that this is the plain score of something which can take on its full life only with the living voice. In an average year of academic lecturing it is not unusual to utter about two million words, most of them extempore, but I write, as my friends know, unwillingly and uneasily. I am not sufficiently practised a writer to convey a vocal pattern with exactness, and I have always admired Miss Gertrude Stein, whose lecture on "Composition as Explanation" is the most perfect broadcast script I know. I have made no attempt to write for anyone's voice but my own, and I hope those who heard the broadcasts will supplement the text with their recollections.

As a literary historian I have tried to treat contemporary literature as seriously as I would Elizabethan or Augustan writing, bearing in mind the greater difficulty, that we are too close to the events, that important information, the personal and secondary information which helps to frame the masterpieces, is not yet available. There is, however, the compensatory advantage that so much is alive to us to-day which will be embalmed in scholarly or confused footnotes later. The process and direction can be as clear to us as the achievement, if examined by a trained literary historian. An attempt at assessment must include as part of its material the age's opinion of itself, as well as what it thought of its predecessors. Even errors of perspective may be of some use as raw material. The task of the literary historian is not to impose a philosophical pattern of history on his material, but to elicit, from what to contemporaries is chiefly exciting reading-matter, the pattern into which the more durable productions fall of themselves in retrospect.

It was not possible to deal fully with the remarkable developments in literary criticism during the second quarter of the century, but by quoting so frequently from Mr. T. S. Eliot I have endeavoured to underline the importance of critical standards so reluctantly conceded in the death struggle between publishers and reviewers. The historian belatedly establishes the importance of a Dryden, a Coleridge or a Matthew Arnold. I wished to abridge this delay by emphasising that the creative writing of to-day has been largely dominated or directed by the critical writings of Mr. Eliot. It was also not possible, within the limits of this series of lectures, to give adequate attention to contemporary poetry, but I have dealt with it at length in a previous series of broadcasts on "The Background of Modern Poetry" (G. Bell & Son).

I am grateful to the B.B.C. for giving me a completely free hand in the planning of these lectures, but that very freedom presented a problem, which is essentially the problem of the Third Programme, that of the audience to which the talks were to be directed. There is no such entity as a Third Programme audience. There is only an audience for what the Third Programme alone provides. I did not fully realise how wide and how varied is the public which treks from the Light and Home programmes towards the Third. My intention was to give a map of the country, using landmarks familiar to most people; to indicate to those whose interest had waned recently that literature has not stood still, and to those who are concerned chiefly with to-day that the present has its foundations; to tidy up the chaos of recent years; to recall to listeners concerned with other disciplines what they may have been too pre-occupied to link up with their own interests. I tried to do simultaneously a multitude of things for an infinite variety of listeners.

I am all the more grateful therefore to the many hundreds of correspondents from the widest range of interests, who were kind enough to tell me they had profited from some observation or juxtaposition, some mention of a book or some quotation with a special frame round it, and even to those who complained that they had been obliged to change their dinner hour in order to listen regularly to the series. I am specially grateful to Mr. Antony Alpers for reminding me that Katherine Mansfield said that Van Gogh's paintings at the Post-Impressionist Exhibition had taught her something about writing which was "a kind of freedom, or rather a striking free", and to Mr. Ian M. Milligan for pointing out that Oliver Wendell Holmes in *The Professor at the Breakfast Table* had anticipated in 1860 the presentation of multiple consciousness which is part of the "Stream of Consciousness" method.

The death of Mr. Bernard Shaw came after I had finished, to mark the end of a period at whose beginning his contribution was important. I ought perhaps to have said more of him, but I was not dealing with individual figures, and his main influence had departed when most men would themselves have departed. After *Saint Joan* and *Back to Methusaleh* he was no longer part of the living present. The award of the Nobel Prize to Mr. William Faulkner gives a kind of official backing to what may have seemed on my part a purely personal opinion.

J. ISAACS.

Acknowledgments

THE author wishes to acknowledge his thanks to those authors and their publishers who have granted him permission to quote extracts from the undermentioned books:

H. G. Wells: *Experiment in Autobiography* (H. G. Wells's executors, The Cresset Press, Ltd., and Victor Gollancz, Ltd.); H. G. Wells: *An Englishman Looks at the World* (H. G. Wells's executors and Cassell & Company, Ltd.); John Galsworthy's letter to Edward Garnett (William Heinemann, Ltd.); Graham Greene: *The Third Man* (William Heinemann, Ltd.); W. H. Auden: *The Age of Anxiety; Poems* (Faber & Faber, Ltd.); W. H. Auden and Christopher Isherwood: *The Dog Beneath The Skin* (Faber & Faber, Ltd.); T. S. Eliot: *Sweeney Agonistes; Murder in the Cathedral; The Rock; Four Quartets* (Faber & Faber, Ltd.); Virginia Woolf: *Mrs. Dalloway* (Mr. Leonard Woolf); James Joyce: *Ulysses* (John Lane The Bodley Head); Aldous Huxley: *Point Counter Point* (Chatto & Windus); *The Letters of D. H. Lawrence* (Mrs. Frieda Lawrence and William Heinemann, Ltd.); Isaac Rosenberg: *Poems* (Chatto & Windus).

THE ASSESSMENT
OF CONTEMPORARY
LITERATURE

The Assessment of Contemporary Literature

ON the 31st of December 1950 the first half of the twentieth century comes to an end, and it is my business, in this series of lectures, to take stock of its achievement in literature, and to suggest, so far as they can be seen at so early a stage, some of the directions in which that literature moved. I do not propose to give a formal survey of the development of poetry and drama, fiction and criticism. I want to give a picture of the age as the age itself saw it, and at the same time to indicate how I think posterity will see it. It is the critic's duty to anticipate posterity by offering a judgment, or at least by suggesting a pattern, which a longer perspective ought not to contradict. The material is all there, and I merely want to remind you of the significance of perfectly familiar facts, and the more familiar the facts are the more necessary it is to give them a place in the pattern.

What is so remarkable about the twentieth century, and what marks it off from previous centuries, is the intense awareness it has of its own processes, and its innumerable attempts to describe what is happening, while it is still happening. The Victorians were certainly

aware of their problems and their predicament. As
Matthew Arnold wrote to Clough, "these are damned
times—everything is against one—the height to which
knowledge is come, the spread of luxury, our physical
enervation, the absence of great natures, the unavoidable
contact with small ones, newspapers, cities, light pro-
fligate friends, moral desperadoes like Carlyle, our own
selves, and the sickening consciousness of our own
difficulties," but Arnold never attempted an assessment
of a single contemporary English writer or of any contemporary movement in literature, and his inaugural
lecture on Poetry at Oxford in 1869, *On the Modern
Element in Literature*, had not a word about anything
except Greece. He was preoccupied with the previous
age, the Romantic period, with World Literature, with
"Europe as being, for intellectual and spiritual purposes,
one great confederation, bound to a joint action and
working to a common result; and whose members have,
for their proper outfit, a knowledge of Greek, Roman
and Eastern antiquity, and of one another."

The seventeenth century, a period very much like our
own, was much more concerned with what was happening, and a great critic like Dryden has a modernity we
can appreciate in his awareness of living in a transitional
age, under the towering shadow of the great Elizabethan
period, and worried by the new literary standards of
Baroque France. It was Dryden, in the last year of
the seventeenth century, the year of his own death,
who wrote the epitaph of the century in his *Secular
Masque*:

> All, all of a piece throughout:
>> Thy chase had a beast in view;
> Thy wars brought nothing about.
>> Thy lovers were all untrue.
> 'Tis well an old age is out,
>> And time to begin a new.

One of the reasons why the Victorians made no assessment was that they did not believe and could not believe that an age was coming to an end. It was only in the 'nineties that people became aware of a dissolution, which they called a decadence, and that was associated not with an epoch, but with a century—they spoke of *fin de siècle* literature. There is a curious mystical feeling about the end of a century, and by some accident or coincidence the ends of centuries have been rather wonderful. The end of the fourteenth with Chaucer's *Canterbury Tales* and *Troilus and Criseyde*, the end of the sixteenth with Shakespeare and Marlowe, and Spenser's *Faerie Queene*, the end of the seventeenth with Congreve, the end of the eighteenth with a new world beginning with Coleridge's *Ancient Mariner* and Wordsworth's *Tintern Abbey*. For our own satisfaction, we *must* try to impose a pattern on our time, which means a simplification, and inevitably an over-simplification. Can we pin our faith in dates, and does our age begin in 1901? Does it depend on the deaths of great men? Does our time begin with the death of Oscar Wilde in 1900, or would it be truer to say that the half-century which has a unity is that from the death of Carlyle in 1881 to the death of D. H. Lawrence in 1930, or must it really be the double

B

death of Virginia Woolf and James Joyce in 1941; or does the break really come where Virginia Woolf said it did, in 1910?

Let us be bold and say that our period really begins in 1903 with the "Life Force" as displayed in Bernard Shaw's *Man and Superman* and ends with the death-force, that it moves from the age of biology, which is the legacy of the Victorians, to the atomic age, or that it begins as the sociological age and continues as the psychological era. The new century began on a new note. Victorian solemnity was replaced by an Edwardian, or perhaps more particularly a Shavian friskiness, no less serious but much less solemn. You remember Tolstoy's letter to Bernard Shaw about *Man and Superman*: "The first defect in it is that you are not sufficiently serious. One should not speak jestingly of such a subject as the purpose of human life, the causes of its perversion, and the evil that fills the life of humanity to-day." After Carlyle and Ruskin and Tolstoy a lighter touch was certainly necessary. The chief offence of Matthew Arnold in the eyes of the Victorians was not his attack on the Philistines—not his doctrine, but the tone of voice in which he promulgated it. That too was Oscar Wilde's major offence. *The Importance of Being Earnest* was just as serious an attack on Victorian standards as Butler's *The Way of all Flesh*, but the deft, good-humoured tone was more damaging. Wilde's other offence was taking the art of criticism too seriously. The artist's raw material is life, experienced through the senses, patterned by the mind, and given divinity by that mysterious thing we know nothing about, the soul, intuition, the unconscious, or whatever we like to call it. The critic's raw material is the finished work of art, which he uses as a building brick in the larger architecture of criticism. The present age scarcely gives Oscar Wilde credit for the vast progress of criticism in our time.

It was in 1903 also that the first part of Thomas Hardy's *The Dynasts* appeared. The new century began by accepting what had been fought so bitterly in the nineteenth, the new view of the world as a mechanism, as a process rather than the work of a beneficent Deity, Heaven undermined by science. In his preface Hardy drew attention to "the supernatural spectators of the terrestrial action, certain impersonated abstractions, or intelligences, called spirits" and explained calmly that "The wide prevalence of the Monistic theory of the Universe forbade, in this twentieth century" (notice how Hardy insists on the new century) "the importation of Divine personages from any antique Mythology or ready-made sources, or channels of Causation, even in verse, and excluded the celestial machinery of say *Paradise Lost*, as peremptorily as that of the *Iliad* or the *Eddas*. . . . And the abandonment of the masculine pronoun in allusions to the First or Fundamental Energy seemed a necessary and logical consequence of the long abandonment by thinkers of the anthropomorphic conception of the same." England had already experienced the scandal of Hardy's reference in *Tess of the d'Urbervilles* to "The President of the Immortals." That was in a novel and was noticed, but *The Dynasts* was in verse, and, as Hardy once said, "If Galileo had said in verse that the world moved, the Inquisition might have let him alone."

But the opening words of *The Dynasts* were startling enough for those who had eyes to read. The Shade of the Earth enquires:

What of the Immanent Will and Its designs?

and the Spirit of the Years replies:

It works unconsciously, as heretofore
Eternal artistries, in Circumstance,
Whose patterns, wrought by rapt aesthetic rote,
Seem in themselves Its single listless aim,
And not their consequence.

Here was the æsthetic legacy of the 'eighties and 'nineties casting its shadow from behind, and here was the unconscious casting its shadow before. In that same year, 1903, in Samuel Butler's *The Way of All Flesh*, the unconscious speaks with a very modern voice. It is the scene in the forty-second chapter, when young Ernest Pontifex is being tortured by his parents into betraying his schoolfellows' crimes:

"No matter how awful was the depravity revealed to them, the pair never flinched, but probed and probed, till they were on the point of reaching subjects more delicate than they had yet touched upon. Here Ernest's unconscious self took the matter up and made a resistance to which his conscious self was unequal, by tumbling him off his chair in a fit of fainting."

The twentieth century was being dovetailed into the nineteenth, and striding across the join was the new figure who was to own the new century—the Common Man. The social historian of the literature of our time will be much concerned with the social origins and backgrounds of its contributors, the intruders into the old settled order of middle-class authorship, and one of his chief documents will be what is in many ways the most important of twentieth-century books, H. G. Wells's *Experiment in Autobiography*, because it is the autobiography, not merely of an individual, but of a process. It is an epic of ambition and a parable of modern civilization. It lays bare that strain of inferiority-feeling which may perhaps give this age its historical label, the uneasiness of an epoch of discontent, and that obsession with sex which is the hallmark of adolescent maladjustment whether in a man or in a generation. Wells describes it as "The adventures of a sample human brain in the latter phase of the Private Capitalist System," and more shrewdly as the portrait of "an individual becoming the conscious Common Man of his time and culture." Wells is Kipps and Mr. Polly. He is the Philistine, something far deadlier than Matthew Arnold's educated Philistine; he is the self-educated Philistine, two generations younger than the self-improvers of the nineteenth century. He is the forerunner of the products of the Education Act of 1870. It is the Philistinism of a *nouveau-riche* science passionately condescending towards an ancient aristocracy of culture. He is the prophet of the half-baked and confused, the mirror of the growing-pains of the twentieth century, and his influence on the thought and the literature of the first third of the century is infinitely greater than he has been given credit for. He is transparent and unashamed, and confesses everything. "So much of my life," he says, "has been a prolonged and enlarged adolescence." And on the novel, on its substance and its scope, if not on its form and its art, his effect has been profound.

Early twentieth-century fiction owes two of its main directions to Wells's activity as a pamphleteer and a novelist—the incursion of the theme of sex, and the deliberate extension of the whole field of action of the novel. In *A Modern Utopia* in 1905 he discussed Free Love and Contraception—then called Neo-Malthusianism, and, as he says, "The book was popular with the young of our universities. . . . It played a considerable part in the general movement of release from the rigid technical chastity of women during the Victorian period." His novel *Ann Veronica* in 1909 caused a scandal. "Its particular offence was," Wells writes, "that Ann Veronica was a virgin who fell in love and showed it, instead of waiting, as all previous heroines had hitherto done, for someone to make love to her. It was held to be an unspeakable offence that an adolescent female should be sex-conscious before the thing was forced upon her attention. But Ann Veronica wanted a particular man who excited her and she pursued him and got him, with gusto." The book was banned by the libraries, and preached against by earnest clergymen, and so advertised into notoriety and influence. The familiar ring and animal imagery of the moral reviewer begins to be heard. *The Spectator* wrote that "the muddy world of Mr. Wells's imaginings is a community of scuffling stoats and ferrets, unenlightened by a ray of duty and abnegation." By the time *The New Machiavelli* came to be printed in *The English Review* in 1910 and 1911 a new world was born.

Wells is also one of the protagonists in the battle between the novel as an art form and the formless novel, which is by no means the same as the artless. It is really a battle between the ragged native form and the shapely and purposeful foreign product, what Arnold Bennett used to refer to as "the great Flaubert, Turgenev, Zola, Maupassant, Goncourt group." Wells's attitude was a challenge to the history of nineteenth-century fiction. He was fighting against the conception of the novel merely as a vehicle for character. "In the established novel," he said, "objective through and through, the characteristic exterior reactions of the character were everything and the conflicts and changes of ideas within his brain were ignored." In 1911 he issued his manifesto on the Novel of Discussion. "We are going to deal with political questions and religious questions and social questions. We cannot present people unless we have this free hand, this unrestricted field. What is the good of telling stories about people's lives if one may not deal freely with the religious beliefs and organizations that have controlled or failed to control them? What is the good of pretending to write about love, and the loyalties and treacheries and quarrels of men and women, if we

must not glance at those varieties of physical temperament and organic quality, those deeply passionate needs
and distresses, from which half the storms of human life
are brewed."

Henry James, he said, had no idea of the possible use of
the novel as a help to conduct, so, Wells bluntly said,
"the novelist is going to be the most potent of artists,
because he is going to present conduct, devise beautiful
conduct, discuss conduct, analyse conduct, suggest
conduct, illuminate it through and through. He will not
teach, but discuss, point out, plead and display. We are
going to appeal to the young and hopeful and the curious,
against the established, the dignified and defensive. Before
we have done, we will have all life within the scope of
the novel." This passionate and youthful iconoclast,
this youth leader, was then forty-five. And from that
time the novel, as Wells shaped and taught it, was to be
not character but discussion—it was to be "The Portrait
of the Artist."

Three years later, in his famous articles on "The Younger
Generation" in *The Times Literary Supplement* of 1914,
Henry James in his turn was to sum up the situation of
the novel, to make yet another of the age's conscious and
deliberate assessments. He defines the new as "an appetite
for a closer notation, a sharper specification of the signs
of life, of consciousness, of the human scene and the
human subject in general, than the three or four generations before us had been at all moved to insist on." He
finds Jane Austen wanting in this very special matter.
"Where her testimony complacently ends the pressure

of appetite within us presumes exactly to begin." He finds in Wells and Bennett an inordinate possession of the worlds they present, a saturation, in the tradition of the great master, Tolstoy, but something essential is missing. Each is the temporary master of our sensibility. We are given the *facts* of the life of the Five Towns. "But is this *all*?" he asks. "These are the circumstances of the interest —but where is the interest itself, where and what is its centre?" As a student of form James was superb, as a tipster he was deplorable. In that assessment, among the recent writers he was frightened, respectfully frightened, by D. H. Lawrence, and plumped for—Hugh Walpole!

In the meantime, while Wells was talking, before Henry James summed up, something very important was happening. While Wells was writing in 1911, something indeed had already happened. In 1924 Virginia Woolf attempted yet another assessment, this time of the Edwardian and the Georgian novel, under the title of *Mr. Bennett and Mrs. Brown.* In it she made the startling statement that "on or about December, 1910, human character changed"—a statement very comforting to the student of modern literature, but very few people, I imagine, have the faintest notion what she really meant by it.

The statement is ostensibly about the nature of modern fiction, but in 1910—in December, 1910, as Virginia Woolf exactly dates it—the most important event in England was the opening of the notorious Post-Impressionist exhibition at the Grafton Galleries, where the older work of Manet, including *The Bar at the Folies*

Bergère, and the paintings of Van Gogh, Gauguin, Matisse, Picasso and, above all, Cézanne were seen with a fresh eye. Visitors roared with laughter, the donkeys brayed, as they still do at Picasso forty years later. Only one man was honest, one of the men to be cast aside by the new generation. In that same December, Arnold Bennett wrote: "I have permitted myself to suspect that, supposing some writer were to come along and do in words what these men have done in paint, I might conceivably be disgusted with nearly the whole of modern fiction, and I might have to begin again. This awkward experience will in all probability not happen to me, but it might happen to a writer younger than me; at any rate, it is a fine thought." I can only record the *fact* of this impact of Post-Impressionism, and of Cubism and Futurism and Expressionism, and in a different way, of the Russian Ballet. The actual process is too complicated, and to analyse it we need the still uncollected confessions of those who were influenced, the still unpublished letters and diaries, the records of conversations and discussions, and all the underground material of history.

More direct was the effect of Russian literature, acceptable because it was a spiritual antidote to the materialism of Flaubert and Zola and the De Goncourts. As early as 1909 Arnold Bennett welcomed Tchehov. "We have no writer," he said, "and we have never had one, nor has France, who could mould the material of life without distorting it, into such complex forms to such an end of beauty." *Without distorting it*—notice, this was before December, 1910. But it was the appearance of Mrs. Constance Garnett's translation of Dostoevsky, beginning with *The Brothers Karamazov* in 1912, which started a period of hysteria which lasted throughout the war and shook up English fiction as nothing native had done hitherto. Something of that fever can be seen in Mr. Middleton Murry's biography of Dostoevsky in 1916, and in parts of his *Evolution of an Intellectual* after the war, and something of the resistance can be seen in John Galsworthy, who represented the vested interests of the English tradition of the novel— modified strongly by the other Russian, the gentler Russian, the French Russian, Turgenev. In 1914 Galsworthy was not the fictional ambassador to Europe he became in 1922 with the completion of *The Forsyte Saga*, and another part of the battlefield can be seen in his letter to Edward Garnett about D. H. Lawrence's *Sons and Lovers* of 1913. Here was the Patrician rebuking the Plebeian, the Patrician who had sent Garnett "a list of one hundred and thirty upper-class men and women he had met and known" to prove that he really was at home with the aristocracy.

"I've finished *Sons and Lovers*," he wrote in 1914. "I've nothing but praise for all the part that deals with the mother, the father and the sons; but I've a lot besides praise for the love part. . . . It's not good enough to spend time and ink in describing the penultimate sensations and physical movements of people getting into a state of rut; we all know them too well. There's genius in the book, but not in that part of the book. The body's never worth

while, and the sooner Lawrence recognizes that the
better—the men we swear by, Tolstoy, Turgenev,
Tchehov, Maupassant, Flaubert, France, knew that truth;
they only use the body, and that sparingly, to reveal the
soul." But the cry from the heart comes in the Postscript:
"PS. Confound all these young fellows; how they have
gloated over Dostoevsky."

With Dostoevsky literature plunged into profundities
hitherto unknown, instructive, intuitive profundities,
below the surface of consciousness. The door to the
unknown was being pushed open. The known surface
of man had seemingly been explored to exhaustion—the
naturalist approach, the realist approach, the sociological
approach. The biological, the financial and political
organization of man, the obvious springs of love had been
examined, and overcropping had produced a kind of
dust-bowl in the landscape of fiction. It remained only
for science to give its sanction to the exploration of the
remainder of human feeling, the submerged iceberg of
the unconscious.

If, as I have suggested, the twentieth century may be
said in one way to begin with the "life-force" which
Bernard Shaw compounded out of the theories of Berg-
son and of Samuel Butler, in another way it can be said
to begin with the publication of Sigmund Freud's
Interpretation of Dreams in 1900. But not yet in England.
Once again the year 1910 becomes significant, when
Freud's own account of the development and subject-
matter of psycho-analysis was published in *The American
Journal of Psychology*. The *Interpretation of Dreams* was

translated in 1913 and printed in three separate impressions, just in time for the War of 1914–18, and with it and with *Wit and the Unconscious* in 1916 and the *Psychopathology of Everyday Life*, which has sold I don't know how many thousands in its Penguin edition, came a tremendous enlargement of our understanding of the mechanism of the emotions, and of the mechanism of the imagination.

Psycho-analysis came in time for the war, and it joined the influence of Dostoevsky. Nobody who went through the war was quite the same person again, and many writers read Freud for the first time in the trenches. Nobody who read Dostoevsky was quite the same person again, and nobody who read Freud could escape the logical and convincing relevance of his theories of human nature and the secret springs of human motives. Where anthropology and Frazer's *Golden Bough* had raised doubts about the origin and nature of religion and the validity of modern social organization, Freud had imposed a pattern on the secret evolution of mankind.

I am neither a poet nor a novelist, merely a Common Reader, and I remember very vividly how it affected me. In 1913 or 1914 I first heard of Freud from a friend who was a medical student. The topic was being eagerly and excitedly discussed by young people. D. H. Lawrence in *Sons and Lovers* in 1913 had written a Freudian novel without having read Freud, though he had heard something about him. Lawrence was being studied by the psycho-analysts, and his friend Dr. Eder translated Freud's shorter book *On Dreams* in 1914. It was all in the air. May Sinclair's novel *The Three Sisters* in 1914 had some tinge of it. When I went to France as a soldier inevitably I took with me in my kit Freud's *Interpretation of Dreams* and Somerset Maugham's *Of Human Bondage*, which appeared in 1915, and I remember that reading them both made me so profoundly miserable that by contrast the war seemed a cheerful adventure. After the war it was learnt that the treatment of shell-shock had confirmed Freud's theories beyond all question, just as the results of the eclipse were to prove Einstein's theories. Rebecca West's *Return of the Soldier* in 1918 was based on a cure by Freudian therapy. In 1920 J. D. Beresford the novelist pointed out "that of all theories of the nature of man ever put forward by a reputable scientist, that of Sigmund Freud is the most attractive and adaptable for the purposes of fiction."

In 1921 D. H. Lawrence wrote on *Psychoanalysis and the Unconscious*, and by 1922 its influence in the novel was on the wane, it was no longer a novelty, it had become an essential and natural part of the modern writer's equipment. Mr. G. M. Young has said that "the arrival of the New Psychology had much of the excitement that attended the arrival of the New Learning at the Renaissance," and Mr. Auden, in his fine poem on the death of Freud in September, 1939, at the end of an epoch, wrote:

> To us he is no more a person
> Now but a whole climate of opinion.

which means that he is now as important as Darwin or

Karl Marx, even to those who have never read a line of any of them.

By 1922! 1922 was the *Annus Mirabilis* of the half-century. The incredible ferment of the years from 1910 to 1914 was bound to produce a remarkable vintage. In 1922 appeared Virginia Woolf's *Jacob's Room,* a "cubist" novel, and James Joyce's *Ulysses,* an "expressionist" novel, and T. S. Eliot's *The Waste Land* a "post-impressionist" poem, and for balance, Galsworthy's *Forsyte Saga*, as a control to measure the speed and direction of the new movement. Galsworthy's was a voice from the past. Virginia Woolf's was a change of direction; she had rejected Galsworthy and Wells and Bennett. In Joyce and Eliot a river had come to the surface which had been running underground for some time. Joyce's *Dubliners* was begun in 1900, but could not be published until 1914. *A Portrait of The Artist as a Young Man* was begun in 1904 and published in America in 1916 because the English printers refused to print some of the words, and in 1917 H. G. Wells reviewed it. "Its claim to be literature is as good as the claim of the last book of *Gulliver's Travels*, and one conversation in the book . . . I write with all due deliberation that Sterne himself could not have done it better." And he said a shrewd thing about the technique. "Most of the talk flickers blindingly with dashes; one has the same wincing feeling of being flicked at that one used to have in the early cinema shows." By then D. W. Griffith's films *The Birth of a Nation* and *Intolerance* had been made, and the cinema had become an art. Wells told Arnold Bennett about Joyce. When

Bennett read fragments of *Ulysses* in the pages of *The Little Review* he was puzzled, but, he wrote, "recalling the time when I laughed at Cézanne's pictures, I wondered whether there might not be something real in the pages after all." When the complete work appeared in 1922 he was won over. "The best portions of the novel," he wrote, "are immortal. I single out the long orgiastic scene, and the long unspoken monologue of Mrs. Bloom which closes the book. The former will easily bear comparison with Rabelais at his fantastical finest; it leaves Petronius out of sight. It has plenary inspiration. The latter—I have never read anything to surpass it, and I doubt if I have ever read anything to equal it." This generosity by Wells and Bennett meant much to a struggling modernity.

If we are concerned with the process of assessment, it is just these things we must know, because in all the arts, but especially in literature, there is the producer and the consumer. All our literary histories concentrate on the producer, on the goods offered and the goods which sold and continue to sell. What we need very badly is a consumer's history of literature, of the tastes and sales-resistances, of the crazes and fashions, of the state of the market, and of the publicity campaigns, the actual sales figures and the profits, and the mergers and manœuvres, of the fight between the multiple stores and the little men, between book societies and literature, of the cheap editions and floating opinion, and even of the crashes and bankruptcies and remainders.

Much of the material for this exists, unless it has been

sent for salvage, in that phenomenon of the twentieth century, the "Little Reviews." They take their name from *The Little Review* of New York, which fought so fiercely for the publication of Joyce's *Ulysses*. There was the *English Review* under Ford Madox Hueffer, and *The New Age* under Orage. One of the earliest was Katherine Mansfield and Middleton Murry's *Rhythm* in 1911, the first to publish Picasso and to discuss Van Gogh and Gauguin and Croce. There was that most powerful of coterie papers, *The Egoist*, enlivened by Ezra Pound, and later by T. S. Eliot, which published Joyce's *Portrait of the Artist* in 1914 and 1915, and Wyndham Lewis's novel *Tarr* in 1917.

It was in *The Egoist* that May Sinclair praised Dorothy Richardson's novels in April, 1918, and there that I first saw the phrase "the stream of consciousness" applied to the art of fiction. It was there that T. S. Eliot fought for the recognition that important things for English poetry were happening in France, and published his essay on *Tradition and the Individual Talent*. There was Wyndham Lewis's *Blast*, with its fierce mixture of Futurism and Expressionism, and after the war *Art and Letters*, with Herbert Read and Osbert Sitwell, and the swan-song of *The Athenæum* under Middleton Murry, with T. S. Eliot, Virginia Woolf, Aldous Huxley and Katherine Mansfield as contributors.

You cannot have assessment without standards, ruthless standards and ruthless principles, and that is what the new criticism was building up under the influence of Mr. Eliot, whose *Sacred Wood* in 1920 gathered up what had

C

been appearing in *The Egoist* and *The Athenæum,* and the chapbooks of Harold Monro's Poetry Bookshop, and anonymously in *The Times Literary Supplement.* The chief critical organ of the period was Mr. Eliot's *Criterion,* founded in October, 1922. In its first number appeared *The Waste Land.* It spanned the 'twenties and the 'thirties and its death by 1939 was another sign of the ending of an epoch. It died, as Mr. Eliot wrote in a poignant farewell, of the shame and depression of Munich, but it enshrined the critical conscience and the critical consciousness of Europe for two decades.

The middle of the half-century saw the founding of Mr. Edgell Rickword's *Calendar of Modern Letters,* a much neglected and ungratefully forgotten periodical. It may be seen in sample in the volume edited by Mr. F. R. Leavis under the title of *Towards Standards of Criticism.* Its two volumes of *Scrutinies,* also edited by Mr. Rickword, are still valuable, if only for D. H. Lawrence's ruthless and piercing demolition of John Galsworthy. The name *Scrutinies* gave the title to Mr. Leavis's periodical *Scrutiny,* which began in 1932. Mr. Geoffrey Grigson's *New Verse,* which ran from 1933 to 1939, and Mr. Cyril Conolly's *Horizon,* which kept sensibility alive from 1940 to 1949, complete but do not exhaust the list. But I want to make a special mention of *World Review* during the past two years under Stefan Schimanski, whose tragic death in an aeroplane crash over Japan took place in 1950. I want to pay this tribute because he was a friend and a pupil of mine, and because very few people realize how much they owe to his eager and puzzled search for truth amid the Apocalyptic and Existentialist movements of the last ten years.

I have mentioned these "Little Reviews" because they are the foundations of the literature of our time, the battlegrounds of new movements and new ideas, the seed-grounds of all new literature, sheltering the young writers while they are growing, bringing them, while they are new, to the audiences ready for them, and offering them to the commercial world, which will decide their fame or their fate. I have mentioned their editors because one ought always to know who was the literary editor of a paper at an important period, for he has a policy, he chooses the contributors and the critics and distributes the tasks, he provokes creative criticism. The function of such reviews, as Mr. Allen Tate says, is "not to give the public what it wants, or what it thinks it wants, but what, through the medium of its most intelligent members, it ought to have."

To look through a whole file of one of these reviews is to step into a kind of Time Machine. You see what was new and suggestive at the time, and if you look at your own marked copies you can see something even more valuable—you can see what has happened to yourself, for a quarterly number gave you enough ideas to last you three months until the next instalment. Your copies *should* be marked, with the code signs which indicated what was fresh to *you* at the time, and what you proudly knew already. How valuable were those chronicles of foreign periodicals and of foreign literature, how illuminating those generalizations which appeared in the midst of a review of a now-forgotten book, and which appear still in reviews by V. S. Pritchett or Philip Toynbee or Walter Allen or P. H. Newby or Alex Comfort or Edward Sackville-West—and only too rarely by W. H. Auden. That is how a climate of opinion is created, and the very fact that critics are struggling hard to make generalizations is in itself an important mark of our century.

From the picture I have so far presented, it seems as though the first quarter of the century was a period of achievement, and the second quarter a period of conscious stocktaking, not so much of the facts of the achievement as of its inner and essential nature. And we can see this better if we look at the progress of American criticism. In 1925 Mr. I. A. Richards published his *Principles of Literary Criticism*, a misleading title, because it was not about literary criticism at all, but only about the psychological and neurological study of poetry, and in 1930 Mr. William Empson, his disciple, published his *Seven Types of Ambiguity*. These two Cambridge casuists differ profoundly. So far as I can judge, Mr. Richards is not really interested in poetry at all, but Mr. Empson is passionately concerned about it. Between them they instituted an approach which made for the close and intensive analysis of the poetic mechansim; and after Mr. Eliot's essays on the Metaphysical Poets, and his insistence on the "mechanism of sensibility" in John Donne and his followers, and on the "dissociation of sensibility" which took place in the seventeenth century, the whole of serious criticism in England and America was centred on the problem of the poet's response to the civilization of his own epoch, and the function and deployment of poetical imagery. The poetry of John Donne has dominated the critical thought of the last twenty-five years, and even Shakespeare's poetry has been illuminated by these studies. It is probable that no age of English literature has produced such a high level of penetrating criticism, and America proudly claims a large share of it. During the past ten years this has penetrated back again to England, and whenever we see *The Southern Review* which died in 1942, or *The Sewanee Review*, or *The Kenyon Review* and perhaps the best of them all, the nearest we have to a successor to *The Criterion*, *The Hudson Review*, with the work of John Crowe Ransom, and Allen Tate and R. P. Blackmur and others, we are pulled pleasurably up on our toes. It is not merely a critical inbreeding, concerned only with the poetry and principles of to-day, but it goes back to Aristotle and Longinus and Coleridge and Arnold, and continues where they left off, always adding Mr. T. S. Eliot, who is in many ways the Aristotle of our day, or perhaps rather the Dryden, in his methodical formulation of the canons of any form he is exploring. Mr. Eliot's studies on *Dante*, on *The Music of Poetry*, and more recently on the problems of *Poetic Drama* are already part of the history of English criticism.

But what is more interesting and more important for the future of criticism in the coming second half of this century is the fact that the American critics are turning from the deep analysis of poetry to the deep analysis of fiction. There the master is Henry James, whose great Prefaces promise to be the *Poetics* of the novel ready for the commentators of the New Renaissance. John Crowe Ransom and Allen Tate have already done some remarkable explorations which deserve more attention than they have yet received in England. Collections of such criticism, whether of poetry or of the novel, are beginning to reach this country, and I wish I could have delayed this assessment another twenty-five years, because the writing of the second quarter of this century is still a tangled medley. I hope to clear up some of these tangles in the third and fourth lectures of this series, when I deal with the texture and the structure of the more recent fiction. Our perspective is clearer for the first half of the period, as is only natural. We are a little too near to the work of Henry Green and William Sansom, Joyce Cary and Graham Greene, Miss Compton Burnett and Miss Elizabeth Bowen, and even to the later work of James Joyce and Virginia Woolf and Aldous Huxley.

The pattern is clear up to 1930, and that year was in two senses the end of a literary epoch. It was the end of the half-century beginning in 1880, when the contemporary world split off from the Victorian world, and it was the end of the self-contained period of twenty years from the crucial changes of 1910, a period of investigation and probing, of uneasiness and unrest *and* creation, which closes with the death of D. H. Lawrence. Lawrence was concerned with nature as an all-pervading force; he was interested in the animal and vegetable layers of human consciousness. His acute sensitiveness to social atmosphere, his awareness of the subtleties of human relationships spoken and unspoken, avowed and unconscious, go far to justify us in calling the years from 1910 to 1930, "The Age of Lawrence." During the past twenty years Lawrence's influence has been somewhat in abeyance, many of the younger writers have had no occasion to study him, and it may have some significance for the history of the second half of this century that in 1950 the reading public was presented with a million copies of Lawrence's works in the Penguin edition.

In assessing a period of literature it is always important to know what kind of book was available both to the reader and the writer, what new books entered and old books re-entered. We are inclined to forget how much happened in the 'thirties, that it was not, at first, a decline from the glorious 'twenties. In 1930 appeared Wyndham Lewis's *Apes of God*, a satirical epitaph on the æsthetic pretensions of the previous decades, a didactic novel of vast dimensions with something of the same fierceness of an expiring epoch as Byron's *Don Juan*. It was an important work, which he followed up with a critical attack on the new influences from America, Ernest Hemingway "the dumb ox," and William Faulkner "the moralist with a corn cob," whose novels *The Sound and The Fury* and *Sanctuary* and *Pylon* were the nearest to genius this century had seen. England became very much aware of the world outside, of the European consequences of the war, of the Russian Revolution, and of the great American slump. No decade of the half-century was so

generally and universally alive, and for the younger
writers there was contemporary stimulus as well as recent
classics to catch up and assimilate.

In 1930 appeared a translation of the great comic epic
of the war—Hašek's *The Good Soldier Schweik,* a comic
masterpiece which many serious people rank with *Don
Quixote*: and in 1931 Alfred Döblin's *Alexanderplatz,* a
Joyce-like picture of German chaos. In 1930 Proust was
available in a cheap edition, and in 1931 appeared Stephen
Hudson's translation of *Time Regained,* the concluding
and explanatory section of Proust's masterpiece. In 1930
Auden's poems initiated a new movement in poetry,
away from the symbolist and towards social comment.
John Das Passos, Robert Cantwell, Albert Halper and
other American proletarian novelists explored social
structure, man, not as an individual, but as part of the
social process. A flood of translation from the Russian
culminated in the inevitable best-seller, Sholokhov's
Quiet Flows the Don, which filtered the doctrines of
socialist realism and softened them to the larger masses.
Christopher Isherwood presented the debris of the fixed
and ordered world of Berlin which was soon to pass.
Graham Greene dealt with the physical and spiritual
shabbiness of the present world, and Aldous Huxley
demolished even the hopeful future in *Brave New World.*
Joyce's *Ulysses* was still proscribed, and was not published in this country until 1936, but in 1930 anybody
with a shilling to spare could buy his *Anna Livia Plurabelle,*
and in 1936 Faber's *Book of Modern Poetry,* edited by
Michael Roberts, made it clear to the ordinary reader

that a new movement in poetry had begun—three new movements, to be exact: the worlds of Auden, of Dylan Thomas, and of Surrealism. There was Franz Kafka's *The Castle* and *The Trial*. In drama there was T. S. Eliot's *Sweeney Agonistes*, *The Rock*, *Murder in the Cathedral* and *The Family Reunion*, and the plays of Auden and Isherwood. Hitler, Spain, Munich. *The Criterion* was dead by 1939. *Finnegans Wake* was published in 1939, and so ended another epoch. After that, all is confused. We are back where we began, with Matthew Arnold again, "the height to which knowledge is come, newspapers, cities, our own selves, and the sickening consciousness of our own difficulties."

I have tried to give you a panoramic view of the half-century—or at any rate of four-fifths of it, the skeleton without the flesh. Under the title of *The Age of Anxiety* I shall scrutinize in close-up the puzzling decade of the 'forties. I hope we are not *too* close to it. It has taken us 300 years to sum up the first half of the seventeenth century—an age, like ours, of psychology and criticism, of science and politics and tough poetry. Is it too soon to hold an inquest on the twentieth century? The corpse is not officially dead until the 31st of December!

II

THE AGE OF ANXIETY

The Age of Anxiety

IN the opening lecture of this series I tried to set out the pattern of this half-century's progress in literature. The impression I wanted to give was: that we know where we are as far as 1930, that we have a fairly good idea of the highlights of the 'thirties, and that we are almost completely puzzled about the 'forties. We are still in the middle of the process which began or was interrupted in 1939, the year which saw the publication of James Joyce's *Finnegans Wake* and James Hadley Chase's *No Orchids for Miss Blandish*.

An epoch is known by the catch words it bandies about, whether they represent a real epit... f the time or only a fancied malady. The seventeenth ... was concerned with "reason," the eighteenth cent... "nature," and our concern is with "the human pr..." Our own preoccupations are shown by the fre... h which we talk of frustration, bewilderment, m... nt and disintegration, the intensity with which we discuss and are aware of cruelty, violence and sadism, the all-pervading sense of anxiety, and in the background a feeling of guilt, sin, humiliation and despair. Never faith, hope or charity.

These are all symptoms of a psychological and spiritual

malady, not confined to a number of unhappy and disturbed individuals such as we find in all epochs, but a collective malady. It is not confined to England alone; it is a world sickness. Among the drawings of Albert Dürer there is a self-portrait in the nude which he sent to his doctor, with an inscription on it: "There, where my finger is pointing, the spot coloured yellow, that's where it hurts." It seems as though all the sensitive writers of to-day are displaying themselves in the nude, saying urgently, on behalf of humanity, as great writers have always done, "That's where it hurts." They are not hiding their agonies bravely, with a pretence of cheerfulness and health, pretending to change the subject, like Boccaccio in his *Decameron*. In any sick society, in any plague city, there are always those who boast that they are well, that they are not infected, that they possess a spiritual talisman which isolates them. If they happen to survive they say "I told you so," and there are many writers to-day who ignore the plague and complain bitterly of what they call "abnormality, morbidity, pessimism, self-pity, and squalor."

During the past year, the last year of our half-century, I have noticed an increase in the complaints against the mood of the 'forties. The malcontents are plucking up courage as though they feel that the tide is with them. They fall tooth and nail on the two chief culprits, Kafka and Kierkegaard. The complaints seem to be of two kinds. First, that it's all too high-brow for the plain man, "Give us character, not symbols, give us stories, not allegories." The second is that it's no longer in the height of fashion, it's *vieux-jeu.* "Angst" is out of fashion,—after all it's only the German for anxiety-neurosis. And then, over-riding all, comes the real protest: it's all so un-English, it's Danish, or—worst and safest of all insults—it's Central European. "This concern with man's destiny is so morbid," they say; "it reminds us of the prophets of the Old Testament, it's as pessimistic as Job—and all this concern with man's relation to God, and original sin, it's all too much like the New Testament. And all this worrying about the individual and the state, it's just a hangover from the old-fashioned leftish 'thirties."

All this quite clearly marks the turning of a tide. Its very confusion is an index of the confused state of an age of transition, and its very existence is just as much a part of the literary history of our time as the literature it is condemning and by so doing, assessing. John Stuart Mill as a young man in 1831 wrote an essay on "The Spirit of the Age," on the notion of a "Zeitgeist" as the dominant idea of his time, which he called "an age of transition." "In all other conditions of mankind," he wrote, "the uninstructed have faith in the instructed. In an age of transition, the divisions among the instructed nullify their authority, and the uninstructed lose their faith in them." That is exactly our situation. But the division among the instructed to-day is simpler and more fundamental. It is between those who see that there is a malady, and those who refuse to see it.

I am afraid it is no use saying that the pains are all imaginary, that there is nothing to fear, to be anxious about, to dread. This is *The Age of Anxiety*, as Mr. Auden calls it in the title of his poem, and every one of us can bear individual witness. We have all been tortured by sadistic schoolmasters, as Mr. Graham Greene points out. We have all suffered from the frown of the boss and the fear of the sack, as Jonathan Swift once suffered. One of the most remarkable things in his *Journal to Stella* is the rebuke Swift administered to Mr. Secretary Harley: "One thing I warned him of, never to appear cold to me, for I would not be treated like a schoolboy, that I had felt too much of that in my life already." And the next day he is still brooding on it: "Don't you remember how I used to be in pain when Sir William Temple would look cold and out of humour for three or four days, and I used to suspect a hundred reasons? I have pluckt up my spirit since then, faith: he spoiled a fine gentleman." It had rankled for nearly twenty years, and was never to be eradicated, and in the end it produced *Gulliver's Travels*. Now, in the new world of bureaucracy, there is a new fear, the fear of the secret and adverse report, and the fatal rumour of political unreliability. An American novel like Merle Miller's *The Sure Thing* gives an ominous picture of this new kind of brooding anxiety.

But it is not only at this low level of personal and economic insecurity, however profound and lasting the effects, that anxiety affects literary creation. It is at the far deeper level of the individual's instability in relation to the universe and to God, his insignificance in relation to the new pattern of science, which is changing at such a dizzy rate, and his consequent inability to decide on a religion, or even to allow, with equanimity, the decision to be made for him. Of course we'll recover, other ages have recovered, but it doesn't make the pain less real. Later historians will record dispassionately that between 1930 and 1950, that infinitesimally short period, English literature had a slight indisposition, felt a slight malaise. They may even notice that there was also a slight Continental influenza. It is all the more necessary then that we who are feeling the malaise, who are in fact suffering agony, should record the symptoms, for the possible benefit of all future sufferers.

We are not the first epoch to feel puzzled, confused and anxious, but we are, I think, the first to be pervaded by a feeling of guilt, an uneasy and nameless guilt. The seventeenth century had a very specific reason for its bewilderment. It was caught up at last by the Copernican explosion. After a time-lag of about three-quarters of a century, the contributions of Kepler and Galileo, the discovery of new stars in a supposedly fixed universe, made the problem actual, and forced modern man to face the implications of the Copernican view. The platform of man's beliefs collapsed. His self-confidence was sapped. His self-importance was undermined. He was no longer the glorious summit of God's creation, set in the very centre of the universe. There might be other worlds, with other, possibly superior, inhabitants. It is a fashion among literary historians to say that such a recognition was not widespread, that it had no more effect then than Einstein's theories have on the common man to-day. But we are not talking about the common man. The

D

point is that the recognition was made by the pioneers, and not by the camp-followers, whose simple thinking on the old lines lasted another 200 years, until Darwin administered the next shock. It was not necessary for the poets to accept the new scientific doctrines, it was sufficient for them to be aware of them and to be worried by them. John Donne was a man who made poetry out of his anxiety, and that is why he appeals so much to our own struggling, anxious age. That he was himself personally insecure and anxious, on economic, religious and sexual grounds, does not minimize or explain away his contribution. On the contrary, it makes it the more valuable and instructive to us. He wrote on suicide, and in his *First Anniversary* he spoke of "this world's general sickness," and our most familiar quotation from him, apart from "for whom the bell tolls," is the description of the devastating effect of the new science.

> The new philosophy calls all in doubt:
> The element of fire is quite put out;
> The sun is lost, and th' earth, and no man's wit
> Can well direct him where to look for it.
>
> .   .   .   .   .
>
> 'Tis all in pieces, all coherence gone.

In the poetry of Yeats and of Auden, there are many echoes of the music and substance of Donne. "The centre cannot hold," "The stars are dead, The animals will not look."

And it was Mr. Eliot who reminded this century of

another obsession which it shares with the early seventeenth century, the obsession with death:

> Webster was much possessed by death
> And saw the skull beneath the skin.

Death has forced his attentions on our century with
increasing insistence. Freud in his analysis of the "death-
wish" has suggested that mankind is "half in love with
easeful Death," and in so far as the "death-wish" is in
conflict with the "life-force" it has become a potent
ingredient in the anxiety of the age. Worse than death
even is death in life. Where the nineteenth century feared
that spiritual death which comes from the loss of religious
faith, the twentieth century fears that death in life which
is the loss of sexual potency. The fundamental anxiety
of mankind about the atomic bombs is not the fate of
those who are lucky enough to be killed, but the sterili-
zation of those who survive. The most ominous official
statement I have ever read is the reassuring advice of the
Atomic Energy Commission: "Persons exposed to
radiation should refrain from begetting offspring for a
period of two to three months." With such material for
nightmare, is it surprising that the poet and the novelist
should suffer from terror-dreams, and that literature,
when it does not report such fears directly, should present
them in symbolical or allegorical forms?

We know now what dreams are. They may be simple
things, "th' imagery of our day desires," childish wish-
fulfilments such as "From mill-girl to marchioness" or
"She married her boss," or more adult ones like Thomas

More's *Utopia*. They may be fantastic structures in code to baffle the censor, such as Ernst Jünger's *The Marble Cliffs*, though he must have been a poor censor not to see through such a simple code. Or they may be easily unravelled parables, such as Bunyan's *Pilgrim's Progress*, or difficult ones like Kafka's *The Castle* or *The Trial*. The main thing is that in this kind of fairy tale an individual, or ordinary average individual, shall be selected to represent the predicament of mankind in the particular circumstances under consideration, and that the reader shall be invited to identify himself with that individual. It is interesting that the three great fairy tales which appeared on the threshold of the modern novel were all of this kind—*Pilgrim's Progress*, *Robinson Crusoe* and *Gulliver's Travels*, a religious, an economic and an intellectual parable.

The simple reader doesn't want parables. He wants simple stories of love and battle—and he gets them still at the cinema in the simple films of "kiss-kiss and bang-bang." The serious reader, however, is worried, and the serious writer is worried. They want to meet and talk about their problem. The worry is vague, the anxiety undefined, so that it is necessary to find out first what the problem is, before it can be solved. They explore. "Man's life is like a journey," suggests Homer, and writes his parable on this pattern. But the *Odyssey* is not an aimless journey. In the opening book, near the beginning of the story, the text is stated clearly when Zeus says, "What a lamentable thing it is that men should blame the gods and regard *us* as the source of their troubles, when it is their own wickedness that brings them sufferings worse than any which Destiny allots them." A modern writer like Patrick Bair says, "Man's life is like a journey, a journey in a train," and instead of sin as the pattern he takes the social order, the class system. He puts the ruling classes in the first-class coaches, and the workers in the third-class, an obvious parable, with the train hurtling along, round and round on a circular track, aimlessly and endlessly. Like all these books it is a thriller, and there is a revolution and a disruption. Patrick Bair calls his book *Faster, Faster*. It has a double, parallel excitement, with all the thrill of those entertainment films in which international spying and adventure takes place on a *train de luxe*, and it has all the parable of Ilya Trauberg's Russian film *The Blue Express*, in 1929, fighting its way through China in a struggle between Communism and Capitalism.

The analogies pile up in a desperate attempt to understand, to soften the agony by rubbing one's nose in it. There are Rex Warner's allegories, dealing with power and dictatorship. *The Aerodrome, The Wild Goose Chase, Men of Stone,* and *The Professor* who meets his fate, "shot while attempting to escape." This kind of story is the novel written to a thesis, whether the theme be the one quoted by Graham Greene from Cardinal Newman, "Either there is no Creator, or this living society of man is in a true sense discarded from His presence. . . . *If* there be a God, *since* there is a God, the human race is implicated in some terrible aboriginal calamity," or whether the text is the one taken by Rex Warner from the sixth chapter of the Epistle to the Ephesians: "For our contention is not with the blood and the flesh, but with dominion, with authority, with the blind world rulers of this life, with the spirit of evil in things heavenly." Whether the story be of gangsters or dictators, pure entertainment or political allegory, the dividing line is very thin. In the original story on which Graham Greene's film of *The Third Man* was made, there are many important confessions which cannot appear in a pure entertainment. "They were one of a group," he writes, "and if there was guilt, the leaders bore the guilt. A racket works like a totalitarian party." And the dizzying muddle of religion, politics and crime stands out in Harry Lime's words, "In these days nobody thinks in terms of human beings. Governments don't, so why should we? They talk of the people and the proletariat, and I talk of the mugs. It's the same thing. They have their five-year plan and so have I." "You used to be a Catholic." "Oh, I still *believe*, old man, in God and mercy and all that. I'm not hurting anybody's soul by what I do." It is this same treatment of mugs that we find in Ben Jonson's dramatic thrillers, *Volpone* and *The Alchemist*.

H. G. Wells once pointed out that the earlier novel was produced in an atmosphere of security, for the entertainment of secure people who liked to feel established and safe for good. Nowadays the novel is produced in an atmosphere of insecurity, for the further mortification of those who wish their agonies of insecurity to be perpetuated. Instead of being an entertainment, the serious novel is a continual rubbing of salt in the wound. It cannot therefore continue to be a report, a direct description or an enumeration of details as it was in Galsworthy or Bennett, and as it still is in the simple tale-tellers of to-day. The novel of the past two decades, faced with the problem of recording the breakdown of a settled and established order, has been led by the example of modern poetry to adopt what is essentially the poetic method. The method of implication, of metaphor and of symbol, the method of splintered symbolism, as in Mr. Eliot's *Prufrock* and *The Waste Land,* as opposed to the descriptive directness of Mr. Masefield's *Everlasting Mercy* and *The Widow in the Bye Street.* The special symbol it has chosen, a symbol which occurs time and time again in the oblique novel, is the symbol of seediness. Seediness, shabbiness and squalor, these are the pervading atmospheres, and the healthy impatient critic does well to complain of the all-pervading presence of these three things in modern fiction, because in so doing he admits and advertises their significance, which might otherwise be lost in the plain fact of their existence. The mistake that such criticism makes, the confusion under which it labours, is to suppose that the mind of the novelist himself is sordid, that he imposes the colour of his own mind on the whole world, whereas it is the whole world which has forced this colouring on the novelist's mind.

Seediness is the mark of a world that has seen better days. I remember being shocked by the shabbiness of defeat in Vienna—gay Vienna—when I first saw it in 1925. The peeling stucco of great mansions, the flaking paint of palaces. Seediness can be used as a symbol of the disintegration of a civilization, or it can stand for spiritual degradation, the sourness of a society, as it sometimes does in D. H. Lawrence. In Graham Greene's novels there is a deliberate philosophy of seediness; he recurs to it time and time again, it is one of his favourite words. In his *Journey without Maps* in Liberia he says: "There seemed to be a seediness about the place you couldn't get to the same extent elsewhere, and seediness has a very deep appeal: even the seediness of civilization, of the sky-signs of Leicester Square, the 'tarts' in Bond Street, the smell of cooking greens off Tottenham Court Road.... It seemed to satisfy temporarily the sense of nostalgia for something lost." It is the same atmosphere we find in the sordid surroundings and the moral squalor of Joseph Conrad's *The Secret Agent,* one of the best of his novels, with an increasing appeal to us, and a book which I feel sure must have helped to shape Mr. Graham Greene. It is the squalor of Mr. Verloc's shop, whose "window contained photographs of more or less undressed dancing girls; nondescript packages in wrappers like patent medicines; closed yellow envelopes, very flimsy, and marked two and six in heavy black figures, bottles of marking ink, and rubber stamps; a few books, with titles hinting at impropriety." It is the seediness of shops behind great railway stations, with contraceptives and accommodation addresses, and ambiguous advertisements written on envelopes. The squalor of Gorki's *The Lower Depths* or Eugene O'Neill's *The Iceman Cometh,* the backgrounds of gangsters either in novels or on the screen, the squalor produced by an army in any house it fastens on. In Graham Greene it is the seedy old-school ties, the men in soiled mackintoshes, Mr. Tench the dentist in *The Power and the Glory*, and Wilson the accountant from the third-rate public school in *The Heart of the Matter*, "who wore his moustache like a school tie." "There was something defenceless in his whole attitude: he stood there waiting for people to be friendly or unfriendly—he didn't seem to expect one reaction more than another. He was like a dog. Nobody had yet drawn on his face the lines that make a human being."

Graham Greene deals with the shoddy people on the "utility" level, and he shares with Evelyn Waugh a moral snobbishness which leaves a nasty taste in the mouth. It is the sick feeling that we get, the sinking in the stomach, in *Brighton Rock* when the priest confesses Rose after Pinky's death. "The old man suddenly began to talk, whistling every now and then and blowing eucalyptus through the grille." It is these gratuitous juxtapositions which produce disgust, deliberately contrived disgust, in Graham Greene, and Aldous Huxley and George Orwell. In Orwell's *1984* the squalor of a destroyed world and the destroyed individual is sometimes stronger than the terror. You remember the cafeteria in the Ministry of Truth. "The metal-topped table on which someone had left a pool of stew, a filthy liquid mess that had the appearance of vomit." This and the shabby vestiges of an earlier civilization where the guilty couple had their love-nest have the force of a philosophical commentary.

The civilization which is breaking down is a civilization of great cities, vast, proliferating cities. And that is why some of the best of modern novels have taken the city as an image of man, in all his richness and variety. It's an ancient image, the image of despair and disintegration in Isaiah and Jeremiah. Proust calls on its ancient associations when he writes of the Cities of the Plain, Sodom and Gomorrah. As a pervasive symbol it is the city of Dublin in James Joyce's *Ulysses*. In Alfred Döblin's *Alexanderplatz* it is Berlin. In Elias Canetti's great novel *Auto da Fé* it is the city of Vienna, and more than a hundred years ago, in a poem that has suddenly become very modern, Percy Bysshe Shelley wrote that

> Hell is a city much like London,
> A populous and smoky city.

The ancient Hebrew prophets, the modern poet and novelist, and the modern sociologist all agree in this identification. In Lewis Mumford's fine book on *The Culture of Cities*, published here in 1938, there is a terrible and prophetic chapter which he calls *A Brief Outline of Hell*. It deals with the creation of terror and anxiety in the inhabitants of what he calls "Megalopolis," the giant city of Western civilization before it becomes "Nekropolis," the ruined city of the dead. He quotes Ruskin on London, and "the appointed destiny of a large average of our population to die like rats in a drain, either by trap or poison." He sees Joyce's Leopold Bloom as a mind "regurgitating the contents of the newspaper and the advertisement, living in a hell of unfulfilled desires, vague wishes, enfeebling anxieties, morbid compulsions, and dreary vacuities: a dissociated mind in a disintegrated city: perhaps the *normal* mind of the world metropolis.'' As an informed sociologist, he calls this the *normal* mind of the city-dweller, and forestalls the critic who considers the modern novelist morbid and pessimistic and squalid in his insistence on selected parts of the city life. What is the normal life of the city? Is it the elegant salon, the genteel suburb, the factory, the office, the stadium, the university, the evening institute, the museum and art gallery, the music-hall, the greyhound track or the church? Is it the thieves' kitchen, the café, the beer-garden, the milk-bar or the corner house, or is it the lying-in hospital or the laying-out parlour, the brothel, the public lavatory, the prison, or the sewer? Some of these parts of the city have entered as symbols into the novels of Henry Green and James Joyce, Graham Greene and Alex Comfort. The chase in the sewer is now a symbolic part of the film thriller, and very recently appeared in *The Third Man*. The topography of Hell and its interior decoration is a very great concern of the modern drama-tist and the modern novelist. In Jean-Paul Sartre's play *In Camera* Hell is a room in a hotel, with Second Empire furniture and sofas and a dated hideous bronze ornament on the mantelpiece, no bed, no window, no mirror, and the lights perpetually on. Hell is particularly memorable in Anthony West's remarkable novel *On a Dark Night*, and among the poets it is Mr. Eliot who has familiarized us with:

> restless nights in one-night cheap hotels
> And sawdust restaurants with oyster-shells

and with basement kitchens and "the damp souls of housemaids Sprouting despondently at area gates" and:

> Over buttered scones and crumpets
> Weeping, weeping multitudes
> Droop in a hundred A.B.C.'s.

In France the best recent allegory of man's resistance against the power of evil, and the evil of power is Albert Camus's *The Plague*. The symbol there is again the city—a plague-stricken city, and Camus takes his justification for this use of allegory from our own Daniel Defoe—from that *Robinson Crusoe* which he once described as an allegory of his own life. "It is as reasonable to represent one kind of imprisonment by another," wrote Defoe, "as it is to represent anything that really exists by that which exists not."

The finest book of this kind that I have ever read is Elias Canetti's masterpiece *Auto da Fé*, published originally in Vienna in 1935 and magnificently translated by Miss Veronica Wedgwood in 1946. It has been hailed as one of the great novels of the century, and yet it is hardly known here. It is a book of giant stature, one of those books whose multitudinous intensity sweeps one along in a torrent like the first reading of *The Brothers Karamazov* or Joyce's *Ulysses*, leaving the richness of the detail to be savoured at leisure. Its theme is the disintegration of culture and the degradation of man. In the treatment of evil, compared with Canetti, François Mauriac is a mere amateur and Graham Greene as innocent as a babe unborn. And it is not theological evil. No god appears or is implied in this hell which boils up from the calmest beginning. The story, the surface story which carries the theme, is of a scholar who lives only for his studies and his library of twenty-five thousand volumes, who tricks himself into marrying his avaricious housekeeper, is thrown out by her, lives a phantasmagoric life in the underworld of the city, exploited by a monstrous hunchback dwarf, and in the madness which has been forced on him sets fire to his library and perishes in the flames. As narrative it has the crystal clarity and directness of all great allegory, of Dante, of Bunyan and of Kafka. It is an allegory of the peace of the ivory tower shattered by the incursion of the beast and the bully, raw instinct and brute force. It is a morality tale in which the characters are the purest and most refined of abstractions. For his victim Canetti chooses the most rarefied abstraction of pure scholarship—the philologist—the textual scholar, the specialist in Chinese, the furthest removed from reality, whose world is in the head but whose head has no world, whose activity is pure reason—pure self-deceptive logic. In this *Everyman* of a crumbling culture Pure Knowledge is beset by the forces of Ignorance, Cupidity, Anger, Cunning, Hatred, and Envy, and is beaten to a pulp. Yet everything is sufficiently human for us to take an interest, sufficient for us to feel a guilty complicity and identification with parts of the victim—the victim, certainly, for no figure was ever less the hero of a book. It has wisdom and fairness, lunacy, and comic invention on a grand Satanic scale. I suggest, as an experiment, that you should read it alongside of Joyce Cary's *The Horse's Mouth*.

You may wonder why I have said so little about Franz Kafka, because so many of the books of the kind I have been discussing owe their origin to his two great parables, *The Castle* and *The Trial*. The most remarkable thing about the fiction of the last two decades is indeed the steadily growing influence of Kafka. One might almost say, paradoxically, that the chief English novelist is Kafka, in his many disguises and transformations, with the further paradox that he has produced no English novel of lasting importance. It is an influence which is much resented by the critics of the middle path. They mask their resentment by hinting that he is most un-English, that he mirrors the special problems of a Central European minority. But Dostoevsky is very un-English, and so are Proust and Balzac and Flaubert, and all the others who have enriched English literature. On the other hand, Mr. Auden has insisted that Kafka is important to us because the predicament of his hero, his anonymous collective hero, is the predicament of contemporary man. He died in 1924, but he foreshadows the human situation in the 'thirties and the 'forties. *The Castle* appeared in English in 1930 and *The Trial* in 1937. There is something uncannily prophetic in *The Trial*, the black storm-trooper uniforms of the guards, and the last words of the hero as he is shot. "Like a dog," he says, and we find something ominous in the arrest in the first chapter: "without doing anything wrong he was arrested one fine morning," and in the callous, ruthless intrusion of the warders on the privacy of the individual. When Kafka wrote this it was a huge joke, a preposterous situation, and Mr. Max Brod, the literary executor who refused to burn the manuscripts, recalls how Kafka's friends were in agonies of laughter at the first reading of this chapter, and how Kafka himself was too overcome with laughter to continue. But in 1933 it was no longer a laughing matter, and Mr. Alex Comfort in his novel *On This Side Nothing* epitomizes the age of anxiety in one sentence: "I saw the same fear in her face that I should have felt if a stranger called at night, the world-wide twentieth-century fear which one sees wherever one knocks un-expectedly at any door."

Mr. Auden goes even further. He says "there is no modern writer who stands so firmly and directly in the European tradition, none less romantic or eccentric," and he offers the bold challenge: "Had one to name the artist who comes nearest to bearing the same kind of relation to our age that Dante, Shakespeare and Goethe bore to theirs, Kafka is the first we would think of." He is not so foolish, of course, as to say that Kafka is on the same level as Dante, Shakespeare and Goethe, but if Mr. Auden, who is the poet of the *Age of Anxiety*, thinks that Kafka presents the predicament of our time, I must listen to him.

Kafka is such an amazing technician and describes his

position with such clarity and such precision, without giving it away, creates his mysterious world, his dream world, with such accuracy that he presents a tempting model for all who have another story to tell or another interpretation to offer for his parable. His problem is so intensely felt and presented that it becomes Everyman's problem. Every man may apply Kafka's general pattern to his own immediate problem. If you are interested in original sin, then the stories are about original sin. If you are the eternal modern exile trying to find a place in a settled land, whether of the body or the spirit, then the story is about that. If you hate the law and think, like Dickens, that life is a trial in a Circumlocution Court, then the book is about that. If your problem is the search for God, the book is about the search for God. It is a pattern of argument, a tone of voice, even a syntax of exploration. That is why it was so useful in the early poetry of Mr. Auden, and why it was so useful in the early work of Mr. William Sansom, who took over and applied very successfully the method of some of the great shorter pieces, such as *The Metamorphosis*. It is more than probable that Kafka's world-picture arose from a personal neurosis, but this personal neurosis happens to have become the neurosis of the age of anxiety, of civilized society in what has been called the apocalypto-technic age, the age of explosives.

Kafka has been seized on by the Existentialists as a link in the chain with Kierkegaard. I am not a philosopher and I do not know what Existentialism is, though I have been told many times, nor do I know what Shakespeare's philosophy was, but if Existentialism is responsible for the quality of some of the plays and novels of Albert Camus and Jean-Paul Sartre, and if it is responsible for the salvaging of Søren Kierkegaard as a fresh stimulus to modern despair, I am grateful. For Kierkegaard is a man of insights as profound and as witty as Nietzsche's. He is yet another prophetic genius, and a hundred years ago knew all about our predicament, our age of anxiety. In fact, he invented it. He knew about the function of the informer, the stool-pigeon, the police-spy in a police state. "The Police-Spy," he wrote, "a demoniacal figure, who could just as well have been dissolute, even a murderer, but is actually in the service of justice (a childhood and youth full of failures has made him spiteful towards mankind). Had I followed my pleasure," he says blandly, "and chosen what I plainly have a decided talent for: police-spy, I should have been much happier than I afterwards became." He knew all about the death-wish before Freud was born, the sickness unto death. "Dread is a desire for what one dreads, a sympathetic antipathy. One fears, but what one fears one desires." He reinforced the notion of original sin and singlehanded he investigated *The Concept of Dread*. He is the grandfather of modern anxiety, as Kafka is its father. Kafka came to us in 1930. Kierkegaard had to wait till the eve of the 'forties, and *The Concept of Dread* was translated only as recently as 1944.

The weight of modern anxiety is compounded of a strange medley of guilt. It has been suggested that the modern process began with the guilt of the Industrial

E

Revolution, and the guilt about the poor engendered by the growth of money. It is this which peers through the whole of Galsworthy's work, but it is recognized before Galsworthy, by Samuel Butler. In his notes for *The Way of All Flesh*, Butler writes, "If a man sins against money, it is the sin against the Holy Ghost," and increasingly, overwhelmingly the feeling of guilt mounts, through betrayals and wilful blindnesses, the guilt about Munich, the guilt of Belsen and Dachau, and Buchenwald and Auschwitz, the gas chambers, the concentration camps and the mass graves, the lampshades made of human skin and the soap made of human fat, and, finally, the guilt of the atom bomb. If there ever was a representative of an age that is now past, it is Miss Gertrude Stein, and the atom bomb caught up with her. The very last thing Gertrude Stein wrote before her death in 1946 was a *Reflection on the Atomic Bomb*, and her reaction is instructive: "They asked me what I thought of the atomic bomb. I said I had not been able to take any interest in it. I like to read detective and mystery stories, I never get enough of them, but whenever one of them is or was about death rays and atomic bombs I never could read them. . . . And really way down that is the way everybody feels about it. They think they are interested about the atomic bomb, but they really are not any more than I am. Really not. They may be a little scared, I am not so scared, there is so much to be scared of, so what is the use of bothering to be scared, and if you are not scared, the atomic bomb is not interesting." If you are not scared! But we *are* scared. In our age of explosives almost everybody is a neurotic, the whole civilized world is having a nervous breakdown, and we are apt to see ourselves the victims of some lurid and fantastic plot, like the nightmare in the film of Dr. Caligari.

Where are we now? We have come down at last from the allegorical heights of anxiety to the world of the plain man. "I like to read detective and mystery stories," says Miss Gertrude Stein. So does everybody. From bishop down to barrow-boy, everybody reads thrillers. If the allegory is the escape-form of the Age of Anxiety, the thriller is the scapegoat of the Age of Violence, loaded with all its sins. Once again we have "The Tale of Terror" as a popular and universal form.

The "Tale of Terror" is not an invention of our time; it arises when there are forebodings of some catastrophe, and it too wraps that foreboding in symbols of apprehension and suspense. It arose in the latter part of the eighteenth century out of the paraphernalia of the Gothic revival, out of the melancholy of Gothic ruins and the vague bogy of Catholic medievalism. It was prophetic of the French Revolution as some of our own allegories were prophetic of the modern terror. The torture-chambers of the Gothic novel, the underground passages and clanking chains, the bandits and secret-tribunals are the equivalent of our gangsters and third degrees, our Gestapos and interrogations, our purges and gas chambers. The Gothic ruins correspond to the ruins of battle and bombing and atomic warfare. In 1794 appeared two books representing the eternal division within the thrillers: Mrs. Anne Radcliffe's *Mysteries of Udolpho* and William

Godwin's *Caleb Williams.* The *Mysteries of Udolpho* is still a readable book, but as a thriller it now seems as ludicrously childish as perhaps our own political "raw head and bloody bones" will appear to the grimmer and more accomplished torturers of the future. Its romantic terrors are more like women screaming at mice, though Mr. Graham Greene is not ashamed to use their technique. But William Godwin's book grows in stature with the passing of time. It is a psychological thriller with a political motive—to depict "things as they are," to show how "the spirit and character of the Government intrudes itself into every rank of society," and to display "the modes of domestic and unrecorded despotism by which man becomes the destroyer of man." It appeared at the moment when Pitt's Gestapo arrested the members of the London Corresponding Society and imprisoned them in the Tower on a charge of treason. "Terror was the order of the day," Godwin said, and he was just as apprehensive of arrest as Wordsworth was later. *Caleb Williams* showed terror exercised by an individual in the spirit of the Government, not yet terror organized by the State. Mrs. Shelley dedicated her Frankenstein to him, and received his condemnation, which is the condemnation of the commercial thriller of to-day, and of that abomination "the story of pure detection." "Your personages are mere abstractions," he wrote to her, "the lines and points of a mathematical diagram, and not men and women. If A crosses B, and C falls upon D, who can weep for that?"

Nowadays, the tale of terror has proliferated in every

direction. There is the political tale of terror, Gerald Heard's fantasies, Arthur Koestler's *Darkness at Noon*, and George Orwell's *1984*. There is the religious tale of terror in Graham Greene's *Brighton Rock* and *The Power and the Glory*, the scientific thriller in Aldous Huxley's *Brave New World* and *Ape and Essence*, the ethical, the existential, the philosophical, the plain detective thriller, and the "tough" novel, and towering above them all in popularity, the sexual tale of terror, *No Orchids for Miss Blandish*. The pressure of civilization and the mechanism of publicity have dulled our responses so that we need greater and greater stimulus, we call "for madder music and for stronger wine." The art of public relations has dulled the sense of private relations, and exaggerated words must be used for exaggerated deeds. The Commissioner of Police announced recently that "Murder, wounding and sexual offences keep up at a disquieting rate," and for the rest of the world England is still the country of Jack the Ripper. The tale of terror is simultaneously the sadistic tale, and has the same divisions, political, scientific, sexual sadism, sadism as a fine art, and some disturbed people have even detected religious sadism in *The Cocktail Party*. The Gothic novel lured the reader with its beckoning titles promising only excitement and suspense. The title of the modern tale of terror is like a tout catering for jaded and impotent tastes. I know nothing more symptomatic than the title of a book I have not read: *Kiss the Blood off My Hands*.

In the schools of English literature of the distant future

there will no doubt be annotated editions of *No Orchids for Miss Blandish*. They will make learned comparisons between the impotent hero of the master in William Faulkner's epic of disintegration, *Sanctuary*, and the hero of this mindless parody, the pallid dictator of the gang, scared that women will laugh at him, complaining of underprivilege, "I never had a plaything, did I, Ma? I never had nothing when I was a kid," and forgetting that he had the habit of cutting up new-born kittens with rusty scissors. They will even find at the end of the book a solemn philosophy which they will annotate from Homer and Boethius and Kierkegaard, "He believed that each person had his or her prearranged destiny to live: that, though the small things come under control, the big things were plotted, like the green holes on a golf course." It is an obscene parody of the Age of Anxiety.

Poetry is more difficult to annotate—except by the poet himself, and Mr. Auden has not chosen to supply the key to his Baroque eclogue, *The Age of Anxiety*, because the age of which he writes is in itself a commentary. But out of our experience the lines leap into italics. "The Night of the Knock when none shall sleep," "The fight with work, the feud of marriage," and the picture of man which Mr. Auden shares with Mr. Eliot:

> crazed we come and coarsened we go
> Our wobbling way: there's a white silence
> Of antiseptics and instruments
> At both ends, but a babble between

And a shame surely. O show us the route
Into hope and health; give each the required
Pass to appease the superior archons
Be our good guide.

As Paul Valéry has said, "Our fears are infinitely more precise than our hopes."

III

THE STREAM OF
CONSCIOUSNESS

The Stream of Consciousness

ONE of the most interesting things about the twentieth century is the way in which the novel has finally become the dominant form of literature. For the general reader it is the only form, and that is why I am devoting so much attention to it. The fight for dominance has always been between the novel, whether in verse or in prose, and the drama. Fiction in prose is a comparatively modern innovation. It has been a long struggle. In the middle ages there was hardly any drama at all, not, at any rate as a form of literature or an entertainment, and the romances and Boccaccio and Chaucer had it all their own way. In Shakespeare's day drama was the great popular form, and fiction was a minor art, except for Cervantes' masterpiece *Don Quixote*. In the seventeenth century the fight was pretty even. Against Ben Jonson and Molière and Racine there was the new psychological novel from France, and a good deal of discussion about the "art of the novel." In the eighteenth century England was leading the way with Samuel Richardson's startling achievements, *Pamela* and *Clarissa,* and Sterne's technical acrobatics in *Tristram Shandy*. In the nineteenth century the novel became a *serious* form, at least in France, and before the end of the century some of that seriousness reached England, in Thomas Hardy and George Moore and Gissing. In the twentieth century it became a serious form in England too—with Henry James and Conrad, and everything that has come since. I am not suggesting, of course, that "serious" is the right word to apply to most of the three to four thousand new novels that appear in England every year. What I do wish to emphasize is that during the past fifty years the art of the novel, in England and abroad, has made more progress than it had in the previous six hundred, and has undergone a revolution comparable with that of the art of painting in the Renaissance in the two hundred years from Giotto to Titian. The speed is astonishing if we remember, still keeping the parallel, that the novel has had to do all that painting did during the Renaissance and all that modern painting has done from the Impressionists onwards. It has had, as it were, to conquer the worlds of perspective and anatomy, of light and colour and solidity, and just as painting did, to emancipate itself from photography. We have got to such a pitch of complexity that, as Mr. Cyril Connolly suggests, novelists "can no longer develop character, situation or plot. Flaubert, Henry James, Proust, Joyce and Virginia Woolf have finished off the novel. Now all will have to be re-invented from the beginning." That, fortunately, is what is always happening in the arts. Cézanne re-invented everything from the beginning, and modern painting, whether we like it or not, has had a fresh Renaissance. James Joyce's *Ulysses* has been called the "novel to end all novels," and it is possible to argue that *Finnegans Wake* went on beyond the end. I think that what we are all waiting for is the Cézanne of the novel to come along and start all over again, but he won't be able—as no great novelist was ever able, to ignore what the great masters of the past have achieved, not merely in their own masterpieces, but for the art they were serving. When we look, for instance, at Rembrandt's great portrait group from Brunswick, recently on show in Edinburgh and London, almost the last thing he did, or the late self-portraits from Vienna, we get a kind of goose-flesh of awe, a tingling of worship, at the possibilities, the subtleties, which lie within the art of painting. And imagine what a painter must feel when confronted with such a challenge, or the challenge which leaps out from the paintings of so essentially modern a painter as Signorelli.

What exactly is the modern achievement in the novel? Before we can answer that, we must see where the modern novelist stands in relation to the great masters, to the great teachers, and we can follow it better by seeing who the teachers were. For centuries it was Cervantes, with his *Don Quixote*. It was *Don Quixote* which gave the European novel its earliest basic lessons, taught it the fundamental analysis as well as the presentation of character, the panoramic sweep and comic invention, the first to impose personality and purpose and relevance to the age on the mere tale of adventure and action. Every great novelist, down to Joyce and Canetti, has worked in its shadow. In the eighteenth century the great master was Samuel Richardson who introduced sensibility and the art of the close-up. In the nineteenth the

two masters who are important are Stendhal and Flaubert. They are the teachers of the modern quality of
detachment, of aloofness, of dispassionate statement.
From them emerged the modern conception of the novel
as a conscious art, and the supreme importance of style.
Not style as ornament or decoration, but style as artistic
and constructive conscience. Robert Louis Stevenson
gives a perfect summary of this attitude in his advice to
the young novelist: "Let him choose a motive, whether
of character or passion, carefully construct his plot so
that every incident is an illustration of the motive . . .
and allow neither himself in the narrative, nor any
character in the course of the dialogue, to utter one
sentence that is not part and parcel of the business of the
story or the discussion of the problem involved." It is
the same doctrine which Edgar Allan Poe preached much
earlier, and which had so much influence in France, the
doctrine of controlled effect. The last of the masters
were the Russians, Dostoevsky with his *Brothers Karamazov* and Tolstoy with his *War and Peace*, masters of
the apparently uncontrolled and uncontrived, masters of
the headlong and the intuitive, of apparently uncalcu-
lated effects.

   The problem of the twentieth-century novelist was the
same as that of the twentieth-century painter. Was the
method to be direct or oblique? Was it to be repre-
sentational and photographic, or was it to be impression-
istic or even abstract? In short, although everybody
agreed that the truth must be told, and reality achieved,
was the truth to be told by means of a lie? Katherine

Mansfield wanted, as she said, "to tell the truth, as only a liar can tell it." Ernest Hemingway said "a writer's job is to tell the truth. His standard of fidelity to the truth should be so high that his invention, out of his experience, should produce a truer account than anything factual can be."

But what is the scope of this truth and this reality? When the French teaching of the nineteenth century fastened on the English novel, George Moore put forward a definition: "The novel, if it be anything, is contemporary history, an exact and complete reproduction of social surroundings of the age we live in." The good novel certainly turns out to be contemporary history, because it is always presented by a contemporary sensibility. But we must ask three questions about this definition—"an exact and complete reproduction of social surroundings of the age we live in." What do we mean by "exact," what do we mean by "complete" and does "social surroundings" include "people"? And, once we have started, more questions come up. What exactly does "reproduction" mean? And what specifically do we mean by "the age we live in"? It is because the new novelists asked such awkward questions, and answered them practically in their novels, that the new novel was born. It is because the older masters, in spite of their genius, did not find themselves faced so urgently with these modern yet eternal problems that the new novelists were forced to make their revolutions in construction and style, in structure and texture. I propose to talk about texture, in so far as it can be separated from structure, which, of course, it can't be in the modern novel. In fact the intimate fusion of texture and structure is one of the paramount achievements of twentieth-century fiction.

One of the great modern pioneers, who is only just beginning to be appreciated as he deserves, is Joseph Conrad. He has been regarded far too long as a freak. He now turns out to have been in the main an important stream of experiment, and like so many moderns his approach is even more important than his achievement. He had the essence of the matter in him. He knew what he wanted to achieve, he knew how he wanted to do it, and, most important of all, he did it. He had a clear definition of the novel. I am sorry to be quoting so many definitions, but, although I have urged the necessity of a consumer's history of literature, it is after all the producer who is important. The critic stumbles along behind the artist and it is good, when the artist does condescend to enlighten us, to have it straight from "the horse's mouth." That, incidentally, I think, is what Mr. Joyce Cary's novel *The Horse's Mouth* is about. Conrad said that the novel is "A conviction of our fellow-men's existence strong enough to take upon itself a form of imagined life clearer than reality." He knew exactly what he had to do: "My task is, by the power of the written word, to make you hear, to make you feel. It is, before all, to make you *see*." He knew also what most previous novelists had failed to do. "Very few of us," he said, "have the will, or the capacity, to look consciously under the surface of familiar emotions." That is why he had to thicken the texture of his style—as Henry James had also done, and why he shook up the chronology of his stories, shifting time about with flash-backs, isolating events in parentheses of time, building up suspense until his characters take on a solidity and depth that are characteristic of the fiction of our century. André Gide's *The Counterfeiters* and Aldous Huxley's *Point Counter Point* take on a new significance if we remember Joseph Conrad's work in narrative counterpoint. In *Lord Jim* and *Chance* he exercises a passionate aloofness which must have come to him ultimately from Stendhal and from Flaubert. He actually records in his reminiscences how the tenth chapter of *Almayer's Folly,* his first book, was begun on board a ship tied up alongside a quay in Rouen, overlooking the very café where the Bovarys had taken refreshment after the memorable performance at the opera.

If Conrad, in the light of later developments, seems modern, how much more so is Flaubert. One of the most memorable things in *Madame Bovary* is the episode at the agricultural show, which no twentieth-century novelist has surpassed, or even equalled. It is an episode made for the cinema, a masterpiece of montage. The scene is set, the "social surroundings of the age we live in" reproduced in all their tense provinciality, and then every device of "cutting" is employed, visual cutting and sound cutting. The pompous speech of the councillor is interwoven with the dialogue of Emma and Rodolphe, alternating in quicker and quicker rhythm as the emotion mounts. There is direct description, there is a tapestry woven of

F

Emma's physical and mental sensations, what she sees and smells and what she recalls and feels. The councillor speaks of pigs and manure and drainage, and simultaneously the lovers talk of affinities and love. The texture is complex, the tempo is heady. At the climax, a climax such as Griffith and Eisenstein have taught the cinema, and the cinema has again taught the novel, "They looked at one another. A supreme desire made their dry lips tremble, and inertly, without an effort, their fingers intertwined." This is precisely what Conrad wished once more to achieve, to make you hear, to make you feel, to make you see.

For one moment Flaubert takes us into Emma Bovary's mind. The twentieth-century novel lives permanently inside the minds of its characters. Let me give an illustration. It is from the famous episode in James Joyce's *Ulysses* when Leopold Bloom attends a funeral, and things pass through his mind as he watches the coffin descend into the grave:

> "The coffin dived out of sight, eased down by the men straddled on the gravetrestles. They struggled up and out: and all uncovered.
> "Twenty.
> "Pause.
> "If we were all suddenly somebody else.
>
> .   .   .   .   .
>
> "Gentle sweet air blew round the bared heads in a whisper. Whisper. The boy by the gravehead held his breath with both hands staring quietly in the black

open space. Mr. Bloom moved behind the portly kindly caretaker. Well cut frockcoat. Weighing them up perhaps to see which will go next. Well it is a long rest. Feel no more. It's the moment you feel. Must be damned unpleasant. Can't believe it at first. Mistake must be: someone else. Try the house opposite. Wait, I wanted to. I haven't yet. Then darkened death-chamber. Light they want. Whispering around you. Would you like to see a priest? Then rambling and wandering. Delirium all you hid all your life. The death struggle. His sleep is not natural. Press his lower eyelid. Watching is his nose pointed is his jaw sinking are the soles of his feet yellow. Pull the pillow away and finish it off on the floor since he's doomed . . . Bam! expires. Gone at last. People talk about you a bit: forget you. Don't forget to pray for him. Remember him in your prayers. Even Parnell. Ivy day dying out. Then they follow: dropping into a hole one after the other.

. . . . .

"The gravediggers took up their spades and flung heavy clods of clay in on the coffin. Mr. Bloom turned his face. And if he was alive all the time? Whew! By Jingo, that would be awful! No, no: he is dead, of course. Of course he is dead. Monday he died. They ought to have some law to pierce the heart and make sure or an electric clock or a telephone in the coffin and some kind of a canvas airhole. Flag of distress. Three days. Rather long to keep them in summer. Just as well to get shut of them as soon as you are sure there's no.

"The clay fell softer. Begin to be forgotten. Out of sight, out of mind.

"The caretaker moved away a few paces and put on his hat. Had enough of it. The mourners took heart of grace, one by one, covering themselves without show. Mr. Bloom put on his hat and saw the portly figure make its way deftly through the maze of graves. Quietly, sure of his ground, he traversed the dismal fields."

I have deliberately chosen a simple piece, without any of the advanced complexities of allusion of which Joyce is such a master. It is a running reverie, a silent soliloquy, the contents of the mind poured out between brackets of reality, the mind in the process of thinking, with its tangled fragments of mental association. Here it is not the portrait of a single mind, a specific characterization, but the mind of all of us—what we all think in such a typical, universal situation. It gives the commonplaces and tags that fill the mind, the clichés automatically evoked. It gives the well-known processes of death and dissolution and oblivion. The sudden personal fears and the callousness and detachment, the grammatical incoherence of mental speech, the dramatizations, the half-reported sentences and quotations, the sudden reminiscences of literature reinforcing the personal unoriginality, the sudden intrusions of fragmentary reality into the self-contained and self-centred mind. And in so doing, by limiting these contents to the average and the unoriginal, it does give a character on a specific mental level. By adding together hundreds of such passages, varying the contents, but still limiting the scope and the level, Joyce creates unforgettably, within the boundaries of less than one day's experience, the figure of Leopold Bloom, the Sancho Panza who is the eternal foil of the Don Quixote who in this novel is Stephen Daedalus, the novelist himself. It is a simple and direct passage. The only cryptic allusions are to two obvious places in literature, the death of Falstaff, and the macabre figure of Sarah Gamp pulling the pillow from under her sick patient. Shakespeare and Dickens, two early masters of this same method of presentation.

Let me give another illustration, softer, mellower, more poetic, more flowing and more feminine than the one from James Joyce. It is from Virginia Woolf's masterpiece, *Mrs. Dalloway*, and like the passage from *Ulysses* it is a reverie, an unspoken soliloquy, between brackets of reality, anchored lightly but firmly to reality. It is an extended parenthesis:

"Millicent Bruton, whose lunch parties were said to be extraordinarily amusing, had not asked her. No vulgar jealousy could separate her from Richard. But she feared time itself, and read on Lady Bruton's face, as if it had been a dial cut in impassive stone, the dwindling of life; how year by year her share was sliced; how little the margin that remained was capable any longer of stretching, of absorbing, as in the youthful years, the colours, salts, tones of existence, so that she filled the room she entered, and felt often as she stood hesitating one moment on the threshold of her drawing-room, an exquisite suspense, such as might stay a diver before plunging while the sea darkens and brightens beneath him, and the waves which threaten to break, but only gently split their surface, roll and conceal and encrust as they just turn over the weeds with pearl.

"She put the pad on the hall table. She began to go slowly upstairs, with her hand on the banisters, as if she had left a party, where now this friend now that had flashed back her face, her voice; had shut the door and gone out and stood alone, a single figure against the appalling night, or rather, to be accurate, against the stare of this matter–of–fact June morning; soft with the glow of rose petals for some, she knew, and felt it, as she paused by the open staircase window which let in blinds flapping, dogs barking, let in, she thought, feeling herself suddenly shrivelled, aged, breastless, the grinding, blowing, flowering of the day, out of doors, out of the window, out of her body and brain which now failed, since Lady Bruton, whose lunch parties were said to be extraordinarily amusing, had not asked her."

This once again is not objective portraiture, but the mind from the inside, the mind allowed to speak for it-self, under minute control but without any intrusion by the author, without comment and without analysis. So it is in the purest forms of what is known as the "stream of consciousness" method, where speech is quoted with-out inverted commas and without labels like "he said" and "she answered," and thought flows, incoherently if necessarily, and illogically, with the special grammar and the special logic of the unconscious. Virginia Woolf differs from James Joyce in making her use of this device a part of a musical pattern. *Mrs. Dalloway* is a musical fugue in construction. *The Waves*, her masterpiece of abstract fiction, is constructed as a ballet with the dancers rendered entirely in soliloquy, endless internal monologues which seem to be direct speech until one examines them, a ballet conducted by the novelist with overtures and interludes poetically and musically recording the passage of the sun over the impersonal sea.

In 1919, when she had only read parts of Joyce's *Ulysses*, Virginia Woolf wrote a remarkable essay on "Modern Fiction" in which, with many lady-like reservations, she praises the scene in the cemetery, from which I have just quoted, as being "close to the quick of the mind." It is there that she gave her famous definition of life, in terms of the particular technique of the novel which I have been discussing and illustrating. "Life is not a series of gig lamps symmetrically arranged; life is a luminous halo, a semi-transparent envelope surrounding us from the beginning of consciousness to the end," and she urges further, "Let us record the atoms as they fall upon the mind in the order in which they fall, let us trace the pattern, however disconnected and incoherent in appearance, which each sight or incident scores upon the consciousness." This is pure "impressionism." It is the doctrine of R. A. M. Stevenson, whose great book on Velasquez was much read in Virginia Woolf's circle in Bloomsbury. Stevenson speaks of "the soft irridescence of the luminous envelope" of "wrappings of atmosphere," of "the aerial envelope," just as Turner the

painter used to speak of "ambient vapour." It is the
impressionist doctrine of Walter Pater also, who has had
a very profound effect on this kind of prose, and on
Virginia Woolf herself.

The Stream of Consciousness method is the impressionist method. Where does this term come from—the
stream of consciousness? It was invented by William
James a philosopher in 1884 and popularized in his
Principles of Psychology in 1890. "Every definite image
in the mind is steeped and dyed in the free water that
flows round it. The significance, the value of the image is
all in this halo or penumbra that surrounds and escorts
it." Here is the "luminous halo" that Virginia Woolf
speaks of. And he goes on: "Consciousness does not
appear to itself chopped up in bits. . . . It is nothing
jointed; it flows. . . Let us call it the stream of thought, of
consciousness, or of subjective life." It comes into the
discussion of fiction for the first time in connection with
the novels of Miss Dorothy Richardson, whose *Pointed
Roofs* appeared in 1915. Dorothy Richardson is the first
novelist to use this method deliberately and almost
exclusively for the portrayal of character, or, rather, the
presentation and creation of character through that part
of it of which the modern world has become almost
morbidly aware. Miss May Sinclair's article in *The
Egoist* in April, 1918, was the first to analyse Miss Richardson's technique. The heroine is Miriam Henderson.
The author does not analyse or comment or explain.
"The moments of Miriam's consciousness pass one by
one, or overlapping; moments tense with vibration,

moments drawn out fine, almost to snapping-point . . .
there is no drama, no situation, no set scene. Nothing
happens. It is just life going on and on. It is Miriam's
stream of consciousness going on and on." This, I believe,
is the first time the term was used about a writer of
fiction.

A year after Virginia Woolf's article on "Modern
Fiction" and two years after May Sinclair had applied
the new label, Miss Rose Macaulay, writing brightly
about a young woman who was thinking of producing
a novel, called Miss Richardson's work "impressionist."
"Perhaps an impressionist novel, like Dorothy Richardson's. Only they were getting common; they were too
easy. One could hardly help writing like that, unless one
tried not to, if one had lately read any of them," and she
gives a parody, with three dots and broken sentences
and all, beginning "Her brain formed phrases and
pictures."

It isn't quite as easy as that, and it wasn't quite as new
as all that. It is impressionism, but it goes much further
back than impressionism, it is the typically romantic
technique. We find it in Scott and in Jane Austen. It's
in all the great eighteenth-century novelists as well—in
Sterne, in Fielding and above all in Richardson, Samuel
Richardson as well as Dorothy. Richardson's *Clarissa*
was written in letter form, and in his Preface he says these
letters "abound not only with critical situations, but with
what may be called *instantaneous* descriptions and
reflections; as also with affecting conversations; many
of them written in the dialogue or dramatic way." These

are the ancestors of the stream of consciousness, the special "close-up" notation and the indirect record of conversation dramatically presented. Richardson's method is ideal for the representation of prattle— feminine prattle above all. Here is a fragment of one of Clarissa Harlowe's letters to her friend, reporting obliquely her sister's comments on Mr. Lovelace:

"'So handsome a man!—O her beloved Clary!' (for then she was ready to love me dearly, from the over-flowings of her good humour on his account!) 'He was but *too* handsome a man for *her*!—Were she but as amiable as *somebody*, there would be a probability of *holding* his affections!—For he was wild, she heard; *very* wild, very gay; loved intrigue—but he was young; *a man of sense*: would see his error, could she but have patience with his faults, if his faults were not cured by marriage!' Thus she ran on."

When the prattle is *mental* prattle, when the mind runs on—then we are very close indeed to the stream of consciousness method.

One of the most remarkable wielders of the method in its primitive form, and one of the least noticed, is Jane Austen. Part of the reason for the Jane Austen revival in recent years is not the refuge her work offers, not the museum quality of her sentimental and genteel world nor its ironic treatment, but the half-perceived modernity of her technique. She has come back, as Conrad and Henry James have come back, as a modern. Almost every ingredient of the stream of consciousness technique can be found in her work: the oblique writing, prattle, soliloquy, internal monologue. There is the incessant flow of Miss Bates, which despite its direct reporting has something of the nightmare feeling of the true stream of consciousness. There is the carefully contrived total report of the conversation during the strawberry picking.

"Strawberries, and only strawberries, could now be thought or spoken of. 'The best fruit in England—everybody's favourite—always wholesome. These the finest beds and finest sorts. Delightful to gather for one's self—the only way of really enjoying them. Morning decidedly the best time—never tired—every sort good—hautboys infinitely superior—no comparison—the others hardly eatable—hautboys very scarce—Chili preferred—white wood finest flavour of all—price of strawberries in London—abundance about Bristol—Maple Grove—cultivation—beds when to be renewed—gardeners thinking exactly different—no general rule—gardeners never to be put out of their way—delicious fruit—only too rich to be eaten much of—inferior to cherries—currants more refreshing—only objection to gathering strawberries the stooping—glaring sun—tired to death—could bear it no longer—must go and sit in the shade.' Such, for half an hour, was the conversation."

This portrait of the collective strawberry-picker is well on the way to montage, and in Emma's agony of self-reproach and mortification Jane Austen is exactly a hundred years ahead of her time.

"The rest of the day, the following night, were hardly enough for her thoughts. She was bewildered amidst the confusion of all that had rushed on her within the last few hours. Every moment had brought a fresh surprise; and every surprise must be a matter of humiliation to her.—How to understand it all! How to understand the deceptions she had been thus practising on herself, and living under!—The blunders, the blindness of her own head and heart!

.   .   .   .   .

"Mr. Knightley and Harriet Smith!—It was an union to distance every wonder of the kind. The attachment of Frank Churchill and Jane Fairfax became commonplace, threadbare, stale in the comparison, exciting no surprise, presenting no disparity, affording nothing to be said or thought. Mr. Knightley and Harriet Smith! Such an elevation on her side! Such a debasement on his! It was horrible to Emma to think how it must sink him in the general opinion, to foresee the smiles, the sneers, the merriment it would prompt at his expense; the mortification and disdain of his brother, the thousand inconveniences to himself. Could it be? No; it was impossible. And yet it was far, very far, from impossible.—Was it a new circumstance for a man of first-rate abilities to be captivated by very inferior powers? Was it new for one, perhaps too busy to seek, to be the prize of a girl who would seek him? Was it new for anything in this world to be unequal, inconsistent, incongruous—or for chance and circumstance (as second causes) to direct the human fate?"

This is so successful, so homogeneous, that it comes as a shock when the author intrudes if only for a fleeting moment into the stream. There is also something very modern in the headlong tempo of this passage.

Brilliant as Jane Austen is, she is still one of the primitives. Her interior monologues are all individual performances, they do not impinge on each other nor contribute to the larger structure. For a remarkable example of building up we must turn to Samuel Butler's inexhaustible *The Way of All Flesh*, the twenty-ninth chapter, where Theobald and his wife are riding in the carriage and the boy Ernest is at home. They all conduct silent and independent soliloquies. Slabs of musing and associations which the author links into a structure without any intervention. It is a different kind of passionate aloofness from Flaubert's or Conrad's. It is something like the technique which Charlie Chaplin uses in part of his serious film *A Woman of Paris*.

The supreme masters of building up are the Russians. Tolstoy and Dostoevsky illuminate their motives and themes by a complex system of searchlights directed on to the mood or situation to be constructed. The same thing happens in the theatre in a play like Pirandello's *Six Characters in Search of an Author*, where the bawd is materialized out of the air by means of the accessories of her trade. Everything modern is to be found in Dostoevsky, even *The Lost Week-end*. One of the strangely illogical objections to the Stream of Consciousness method is that it makes the whole world seem mad or drunk. And conversely that it's all right to use it if you are representing drunkenness or madness, but it's wrong if the theme is normal. The researches of psychology have shown that the same process is at work throughout the whole of normal thinking—that the associative structure supersedes the logical structure even in normality, so that if the novelist is to be faithful to reality he must employ this technique or remain superficial and distorted. The paradox is that straightforward narrative is really the distortion. In 1922 Katherine Mansfield asked passionately, "How are we going to convey these overtones, half tones, quarter tones, these hesitations, doubts, beginnings, if we go at them directly?" The mind flies off at a tangent, the strangest juxtapositions occur, and psycho-analysis shows why they occur. The novelist constructs artificial dreams and artificial streams of consciousness, and they are successful only if they employ the same processes as reality does. There is nothing more mature or more modern in the art of fiction than the end of Tolstoy's *Anna Karenina*. It is quite clear that this is a deliberate and consciously contrived climax. It employs all the modern devices. "Her brain formed phrases and pictures." "There, again it is that girl! Again I understand it all, Anna *said to herself* as soon as the carriage started and, rocking slightly, rattled over the stones; and again *different impressions succeeded one another in her brain.* What was the last thing I thought of that was so good? She tried to remember it. . . . 'No, you are going in vain,' *she mentally addressed a company* of people in a calèche with four horses. . . . 'The zest is gone!' *she said to herself in*

English. . . . No! no! *she now answered herself* without the least hesitation." All this is pure interior monologue, completely unspoken soliloquy interwoven with impressions of the senses, an active-passive process, which differs only from the extremest modern examples of James Joyce and Virginia Woolf, in that the stage-directions are still left in.

The latest and in many ways the most brilliant of interior monologues is in Mr. Hemingway's remarkable new novel, *Across the River and into the Trees*, which has been so lamentably misjudged. Hemingway is giving a portrait of our age, a very unpleasant portrait of a very unpleasant age, and he interrupts the Colonel's monologue with one revealing sentence: "He was addressing no one, except, perhaps, posterity." Posterity, it seems to me, is the ever-present eavesdropper of the stream of consciousness.

Everything modern is to be found in Dostoevsky, I said. I should like to recommend as a superb historical museum piece, his short story *An Unpleasant Predicament* in the volume *An Honest Thief* which has just been reprinted. It is a comic masterpiece, a drunken fugue, and a masterpiece of the stream of consciousness method *avant la lettre*. It contains moreover a conscious analysis of the process, and when we remember that Dostoevsky died in 1881, before William James had formulated his theory, it is indeed remarkable.

"It is well known," he writes, "that whole trains of thought sometimes pass through our brains simultaneously as though they were sensations without being translated into human speech, still less into literary language. But we will try to translate these sensations of our hero's, and present to the reader at least the kernel of them, so to say, what was most essential and nearest to reality in them. For many of our sensations when translated into ordinary language seem absolutely unreal. That is why they never find expression, although everyone has them. Of course, Ivan Ilyitch's sensations and thoughts were a little incoherent. But you know the reason." And there follows a consummate rendering of the stream of consciousness of a drunken mind, revealing character and the social situation of an epoch with simultaneous precision.

How does it all get into English fiction? This was written before 1881, but wasn't, so far as I remember, translated until 1919, so it couldn't have come directly from this perfect specimen. James Joyce says he got it, about 1900 in Paris, from a novel by Edouard Dujardin, *Les Lauriers sont Coupés*, which appeared in 1887. Nobody believes him. Dorothy Richardson says *she* invented it in 1915. I have tried to show that in some form or other it has been in existence since the eighteenth century. And there is one remarkable example, not in England, in the seventeenth. The point is that it appears sporadically and with increasing frequency until the nineteenth century. It is not until the twentieth century that it becomes a regular, continuous and even normal part of the technique of fictional presentation, and in its purest form eliminates all stage directions, all interventions of the author, all comment or analysis.

Joyce said he got it from Edouard Dujardin. I should like to suggest that he got it from Charles Dickens, who is a master of montage and a master of texture. Dorothy Richardson has been called an "impressionist" novelist, and so has Virginia Woolf. Joyce has been classed, by those who know something of the movement, particularly in drama, as "expressionist." Wyndham Lewis in *Blast* in 1914 was spreading the doctrines of that movement. His novel *Tarr* and his play *Enemy of the Stars* have much of the expressionist element in them. In the arts the War of 1914–18 was a victory of the "School of Paris" over German Expressionism, but expressionism has come back as a better technique for rendering a shattered epoch than any other. In literature it consists of splintered fragments and staccato word and phrase projectiles. It is, on the surface, the method of Mr. Jingle in the *Pickwick Papers*, and Leopold Bloom, as critics have frequently pointed out, has much of Mr. Jingle in his speech, but only on the surface. Mr. Jingle is a jigsaw puzzle without depth. Joyce, as Virginia Woolf says, reveals "the flickerings of that innermost flame which flashes its message through the brain," and in *Finnegans Wake* the innermost flame of the whole process of man's history. It comes, I think, not so much from Mr. Jingle as from Dickens's women. The stream of consciousness is a feminine thing, a sublimated prattle of the mind, and it is from Mrs. Nickleby and Mrs. Lirriper that so much of Joyce develops. Joseph Conrad records that his first introduction to English imaginative literature was *Nicholas Nickleby*. "It is extraordinary," he writes, "how

G

well Mrs. Nickleby could chatter disconnectedly in Polish." Everybody remembers Mrs. Nickleby's delightful reverie of ambition. "Closing her eyes, she resigned herself to a host of most pleasing meditations." "Her thoughts flew back to her old predictions." "She gave herself wholly up to the pleasant visions which had accompanied her on her way." "Kate would be presented at Court, of course. On the anniversary of her birthday, which was upon the 19th of July (at ten minutes past three o'clock in the morning, thought Mrs. Nickleby, in a parenthesis, for I recollect asking what o'clock it was)." "With such triumphs of *aerial architecture* did Mrs. Nickleby occupy the whole evening."

"Thought Mrs. Nickleby in a parenthesis." Here in a flash is the whole of Virginia Woolf's parenthetic method, which I have already illustrated. And what about Mrs. Lirriper. I hope, if you get nothing else out of this lecture, you will at least be induced to turn—or to turn back to *Mrs. Lirriper's Lodgings*, one of Dickens's most neglected masterpieces. There you will find comic prattle of supreme accomplishment. There James Joyce found Mrs. Bloom. And this is how it begins:

"Whoever would begin to be worried with letting lodgings that wasn't a lone woman with a living to get is a thing inconceivable to me, my dear; excuse the familiarity, but it comes natural to me in my own little room, when wishing to open my mind to those that I can trust, and I should be truly thankful if they were all mankind, but such is not so, for have but a Furnished bill in the window and your watch on the mantelpiece, and farewell to it if you turn your back but for a second, however gentlemanly the manners; nor is being of your own sex any safeguard, as I have reason in the form of sugar-tongs to know, for that lady (and a fine woman she was) got me to run for a glass of water on the plea of going to be confined, which certainly turned out true, but it was in the station-house."

69503

This is a portrait of a mind, a small mind it is true, but still a mind, on the level of comic prattle. In Mrs. Bloom's gigantic silent monologue which is the triumphant conclusion of *Ulysses*, the sublimated stream flows on through the eternal feminine mind, subtly, without punctuation, uniform and homogeneous in texture, and telling its story with every musical modulation of its memories of Spain, a triumph of technique and a triumph of rendering:

"and the wineshops half open at night and the casta-nets and the night we missed the boat at Algeciras the watchman going about serene with his lamp and O that awful deepdown torrent O and the sea the sea crimson sometimes like fire and the glorious sunsets and the figtrees in the Alameda gardens yes and all the queer little streets and pink and blue and yellow houses and the rosegardens and the jessamine and geraniums and cactuses and Gibraltar as a girl where I was a Flower of the mountain yes when I put the rose in my hair like the Andalusian girls used or shall I wear a red yes and how he kissed me under the

Moorish wall and I thought well as well him as another and then I asked him with my eyes to ask again yes and then he asked me would I yes to say yes my mountain flower and first I put my arms around him yes and drew him down to me so he could feel my breasts all perfume yes and his heart was going like mad and yes I said yes I will Yes."

The stream of consciousness answered a need of the age. It shows "the very age and body of the time his form and pressure," and when we ask what kind of consciousness is revealed we can only answer that it is the collective consciousness of the age, growing deeper as modern consciousness grows richer and more complex. The texture can be thickened as Henry James and Joseph Conrad thickened it, making more and more reservations, adding more and more parentheses, asking more and more questions; or it can be clarified as Hemingway has done it, answering the questions with deft hints until the statements are refined in a pure thin line like Picasso's line, implying the luminous halo by elimination. Or it can present the stream in a rushing, headlong torrent, a swirling mass harnessed to its power-house, meaningless or sentimental or silly if we analyse it drop by drop, where the flow, the flux, the overtones and the counter-point alone are important. This is what Joyce and Virginia Woolf and Dostoevsky did. This controlled texture and tempo are an essential element in the musical architecture of the twentieth-century novel.

By hinting at the nature and ancestry of the stream of consciousness I have tried to suggest some of the growing-pains of the century. Maturity can come only when the process of growing is finished. That is for the future to see.

IV

CULTURE, CHAOS
AND ORDER

Culture, Chaos and Order

THE novel has become the dominant form of modern literature. We therefore demand from it that interpretation of life and of the process of living which we have hitherto demanded from poetry and from drama. We demand from it a view of human destiny and of the human predicament, and, even though the answer comes very rarely, some hint of a solution. Is this too much to ask of a form which is merely a kind of entertainment, or, to speak more accurately, which used to be a kind of entertainment? You remember the claim which Jane Austen made for the novel: "a work in which the highest powers of the mind are displayed: in which the most thorough knowledge of human nature, the happiest delineation of its varieties, the liveliest effusions of wit and humour, are conveyed to the world in the best chosen language."

Mr. G. M. Young has suggested that history is not so much what happened as what people said about it while it was happening. This is a view with which I have much sympathy, for I have always held it about literature. To-day it is not so much what the modern predicament is, as what the creative writer thinks it is or says it is. So that even if there is no predicament, if the anxiety of the age, which I have discussed, turns out eventually, in the larger perspective of history, to have been imaginary, the fact that such a predicament has obsessed the writers of the age and has produced creative work of a high order is in itself a real thing, and will give its colour to the age. If I may take a phrase from philosophy, literature has been produced "as if" there had been a predicament.

The main thing is that writers should have a point of view to stimulate them. It may be a point of view in the form of a definite philosophical system, or just a vague *Weltanschauung*. It need not even be the writer's own philosophy. For *King Lear*, Shakespeare took his philosophy from Seneca:

> As flies to wanton boys, are we to the gods;
> They kill us for their sport.

Proust took part of his from Bergson, James Joyce from Giambattista Vico, from Freud and from Jung. Thomas Mann has confessed that his early masterpiece *Buddenbrooks* is a monument erected to the influence of Schopenhauer. The Existentialists take their philosophy from Kirkegaard and Heidegger, Mr. Eliot perched his *Waste Land* on Frazer's *Golden Bough*, and many novelists in England and elsewhere take the picture presented by Kafka. This is not a new idea. Some time ago I came across a mid-Victorian story which described itself on the title-page as "a novel founded on phrenological observations."

What is in the background of the modern writer's mind, what is intruding continually even into the foreground? During the past thirty years it has been the pervading conviction that we are at the end of an epoch, and the question is always: at what stage in the historical process are we now? Is this the end, or is a rebellion possible, and if so, of what kind? He feels that chaos is here, that chaos is universal, that this is the apocalypse! Once again the position is, not whether it is true or not true, how on earth can we know, but that we believe it and are afraid of the abyss which is opening. The most reassuring thing is to believe, as John Stuart Mill believed of his own time more than a hundred years ago, that it is just an age of transition. The most terrifying thing is to believe, as Graham Greene does, with Cardinal Newman, that "the human race is implicated in some terrible aboriginal calamity," or to believe that there has been some vast betrayal of mankind, to be obsessed, as Mr. Greene thinks Henry James was obsessed, with the idea of treachery, the "Judas complex."

One of the symptoms of our distress, our urge to put order into the chaos, is the way in which we seize on colossal explanatory philosophies, vast "philosophies of history" as they are called, patterns of history. The more artistic the pattern, the more shapely and symbolical, the happier we are.

Recently, while I was undergoing the agony of knocking the whole chaos of the world into shape for this fifty minutes of calm exposition, I asked an historian friend, who is interested in historical catch-phrases, when the notion of "Western culture" cropped up. And he said, somewhat to my surprise, that it was entirely a twentieth-century notion, and that it didn't become popular or important until after the end of the First World War, and in fact, not until the Western world realized some of the implications of the Russian Revolution. My mind immediately leapt back thirty years to the time when Middleton Murry had persuaded Paul Valéry to write two articles for *The Athenæum* on "The Spiritual Crisis" and "The Intellectual Crisis" after the war. There Valéry discussed the problem which was for the first time seriously disturbing thinking minds, "What is Western Culture" and "What is a European"? He puts what he calls the capital question: "Will Europe become what she is in reality—that is, a little promontory of the continent of Asia? Or will Europe remain what she seems to be— that is, the precious part of the terrestrial Universe, the pearl of the sphere, the brain of a vast body?" That was in 1919. In the lecture he gave at Zürich in November, 1922, he analysed the European essence into its three components, Greece, Rome and Christianity, and, as a good Frenchman, gave a picture of an ancient Gaul from Bordeaux who had become an Imperial Roman prefect, writing hymns in exquisite Latin to the glory of the Son of God, who was born a Jew under the jurisdiction of Herod. There, he said, we have the European almost complete. Matthew Arnold's picture of European culture was even simpler, the mingled forces of Hellenism and Hebraism.

Homer has come back, largely through Joyce's *Ulysses*. Virgil has come back, partly through Hermann Broch's gigantic poetic novel *The Death of Vergil*. The Bible alas—the Old Testament at least—is vanishing from the cultural consciousness, with its burden of ethics and equity, the sad heart of Ruth, and Job, and the Song of Songs. I notice its passing, because hardly any Post Office clerk or shop assistant can spell my name correctly. It has come back in part, but only in part, as a useful myth, in Thomas Mann's trilogy of *Joseph and his Brethren*. While Paul Valéry in France was discussing this historical crisis from 1919 to 1923, from Germany between 1918 and 1922 came Oswald Spengler's *Decline of the West* with its sweeping cyclic pessimism to dominate the thinking of the whole world. It was an old theory: Vico had put it forward in the eighteenth century, but nobody had noticed; now in the twentieth century it was topical and relevant and men's fears were aroused. Here was the brink of chaos, and in 1920 appeared a prophetic essay by Hermann Hesse, afterwards a Nobel Prize-winner. It was called *In Sight of Chaos*, and was translated by Stephen Hudson in 1923. It was written in the margin of Dostoevsky. "What I call the Downfall of Europe," said Hesse, "is foretold and explained with extreme clearness in Dostoevsky's works and in the most concentrated form in *The Brothers Karamazov*. . . . The ideal of the Karamazov, primeval, Asiatic and occult, is already beginning to consume the European soul. That is what I mean by the downfall of Europe. . . ." It is a remarkable essay, which ought to be reprinted—remarkable in its analysis of the prophetic nature of the artist, in its observations on the unconscious, and on the Devil, on the chaos and the terror which were to loom increasingly large in the literature of the next three decades.

Meanwhile, the East was impinging on the West, and the remote anthropological past was surging up into the modern consciousness. The battle was being prepared between religion and æsthetics, and for the æsthetic view of religion which is so disturbing theologians to-day. Anthropology was undermining religion. In 1922 Frazer's *Golden Bough* became a new force in its one-volume edition, and out of this ferment and into this atmosphere of discussion emerged T. S. Eliot's *The Waste Land* in 1922. In his recent book on *Culture*, Mr. Eliot confesses that his poetry shows the influence of Indian thought and sensibility, and speaks of the effect of translated Chinese poetry on every poet now writing in English. The whole of *The Waste Land* reflected the chaos which confronted Europe. Its material was chaos, but in itself it was not chaotic. It was the poet's personal order built out of chaos and imposed on chaos. Now that we have learnt to read, we can see that order clearly. One of the great debts which literature owes to Mr. Eliot, and not in England alone, is the provision of a new idiom to present the new chaos of Western culture. It has taken us thirty years to learn how to read a poem.

This world agony had its more parochial manifestations: the "lost generation" of post-war America, and the "disillusion of a generation" nearer home. Mr. Eliot's own comment is rather startling and makes a very fine and salutary distinction: "When I wrote a poem called *The Waste Land* some of the more approving critics said that I had expressed the 'disillusion of a generation,' which is nonsense. I may have expressed for them their own illusion of being disillusioned, but that did not form part of my intention." The East appeared in the last line of *The Waste Land*, and it is appearing again in European literature, largely through Jung's edition of the Tibetan *Book of the Dead*, in Thomas Mann and Hermann Broch, and Hermann Kasack's *The City Across the River*.

It is interesting that Hermann Hesse after the war should see the signs of disintegration and the work of the Devil in *The Brothers Karamazov*, and it gives us some notion of the cross-currents at work when we remember that from 1912 *The Brothers Karamazov* became an integral part of the English mind and of the English novel, and that D. H. Lawrence in some of his more apocalyptic comments was fiercely moved against Dostoevsky. As for the Devil, he works in many strange ways and offers many strange temptations. In the fourth book of Milton's *Paradise Regained*, Satan tempts Jesus with the whole of Western culture in the form of a Third Programme series of lectures on Greek civilization, and the Saviour replies with detailed praise of Hebraic culture. Out of that clash of cultures Milton created the tragedy of *Samson Agonistes*, which partakes of both, and with it he mingled his own personal tragedy.

In the abstract it is Western man we are worried about, in the concrete it is ourselves, men "having no hope and without God in the world." Mr. Auden has admirably defined the modern problem. It is, he says, that of "living in a society in which men are no longer supported by tradition without being aware of it, and in which, therefore, every individual who wishes to bring order and coherence into the stream of sensation, emotions, and ideas entering his consciousness, from without and within, is forced to do deliberately for himself what in previous ages had been done for him by family, custom, Church, and State—namely, the choice of the principles and presuppositions in terms of which he can make sense of his experience." Such a predicament leaves man in a terrible position of loneliness, and Jules Romains in his *Men of Good Will* has portrayed that loneliness with equally terrible power. That is why modern man turns with such eagerness to his contemporaries, and particularly to the contemporary novelist, for guidance.

He is grateful even for journalism, for short-term presentations of his problem, as well as for permanent works of art. Between journalism and the permanent work of literature there are many grades. When the apprehension is raw, the results are raw—sharp diagrams of warning, like Sinclair Lewis's *It Can't Happen Here* for instance, or Arthur Miller's *Focus* with its implied subtitle, "It can't happen to me." The chain is progressive: there is the novel of mere individual man, of social man, of collective man, and then the shift to the higher level, man's predicament, man's destiny, with which is coupled and implied man's religion, man's relation to something not-man. You might establish a hierarchy of the novel, in accordance with which of these attitudes or problems is foremost in the mind; and you notice that the series breaks sharply into two halves. Another fundamental division is between those novelists who work on and with the surface and those who work in depth.

Mr. Edwin Muir, that fine critic, in his book on *The Structure of the Novel*, which he wrote in 1928 (I wish he would bring it up to date), gave a brilliant analysis of the novelist who works on and with the surface, the *Clay-hanger* series of Arnold Bennett, Galsworthy's *Forsyte Saga* and H. G. Wells's *New Machiavelli*. He says: "This kind of novel is not audacious enough to attempt a picture of society valid for all time. To Mr. Wells and Mr. Galsworthy society is essentially an abstract conception, not an imaginative reality; they do not recreate society, therefore, in their novels, they merely illustrate it, or rather their ideas about it." This kind of novel, he suggests, is really a spurious kind of history which occasionally breaks into fiction. He is, in a way, echoing Virginia Woolf's complaint of the Edwardians, and Henry James's attack. It doesn't necessarily follow that those who work *with* the surface of society are working *on* the surface. We can see that in both Virginia Woolf and Marcel Proust. With Proust there is surface and depth simultaneously. He gives first a portrait of the age, then an interpretation of the age, and finally a verdict, an implied verdict, on the age. But, of course, it is not arranged as first, second and third. It is given simultaneously, and it is this simultaneity of impression and expression which is one of the characteristics of our time, and as I hope to show in a moment, the new art-form, the cinema, specializes in this and has taught something of it to the novel.

H

In the series I have spoken of—individual man, social man, and man as a spiritual being—there is not merely a hierarchy, but involved in it there is a pattern of man's development. James Joyce, I think, shows this very clearly. Of his four books, three of them correspond with this threefold division. The *Portrait of the Artist* represents man in his individual, subjective, decadent state. *Ulysses*, among many other things, shows man in his social relations, but with a depth unsurpassed, and *Finnegans Wake* deals, also among many other things, with man in relation to time and eternity and the cycles of being. The fourth book, *Dubliners*, the first one he wrote, is a kind of anticipatory clearing of the ground, getting clear of the romantic mists, in the wake of Flaubert's realism. His whole work accompanies forty years of the century and reflects the floating philosophies of the age, always a little ahead of the fashion and independent of it.

In England, living as we do on an island, we often forget that "no man is an island," and what we think are idiosyncratic productions, and wanton idiosyncrasies at that, are really part of a European process. It is remarkable how close a parallel there is between the work of Joyce and that of Hermann Hesse, an older man whose chief works were published later than Joyce's. The first of them, *Demian*, in 1919, corresponds to Joyce's *Portrait of the Artist*. It is romantic, decadent, psychoanalytic and self-centred. The second, *Steppenwolf* (the Prairie Wolf), in 1927, is an exploration of chaos and of the wolfish elements that underlie the culture of great cities. It can be taken as a parallel to *Ulysses*. The last book,

Glasperlenspiel, in 1943, is Hesse's *Finnegans Wake.* All these have been translated. The same parallel, again with important differences, because these three men of genius are three vastly different personalities, can be seen in the work of Hermann Broch. Broch's huge trilogy, *The Sleepwalkers,* published here in 1932, contains within it a whole philosophy of history, and a conscious philosophy of history. In the first two parts—"The Romantic" and "the Anarchist," set in 1888 and 1903—it gives the antecedents of modern chaos; the third part, called "The Realist," much indebted to Joyce, is a portrait of chaos in 1918, with a running encyclopædic commentary on "The Disintegration of Values." His last novel, *The Death of Vergil,* is again a parallel, with a thousand differences, to *Finnegans Wake.* These are some of the overall patterns of twentieth-century fiction, patterns of order imposed on twentieth-century chaos, the same wherever fiction is adult and abreast of the processes of history.

This lecture is really about the structure of the novel, as the previous one on "The Stream of Consciousness" was about its texture. I am not merely concerned with the shapes of novels, but with why they have those shapes: how and why the philosophical and other problems of the age have forced those shapes on them, and how, in turn, the novel helps in confronting and exploring the problems of human destiny. But first of all a novel has to be written. We don't know half enough about how such a vast thing as a novel comes to be written. Sometimes there are glimpses, sometimes the novelist's plans have survived, and have been published: Galsworthy's plans for *The Forsyte Saga*, George Eliot's "Quarry," as she called it, for *Middlemarch*. Balzac and Zola have left important material, and there is a remarkable plan of an unwritten novel by Dostoevsky. We know something of the agonies of James Joyce in shaping his masterpieces. The serious novelist is an artist, a conscious artist, not a mere tale-spinner.

One of the reproaches against the arts in this age of ours is that the artist has discarded his sacred detachment and allowed us to wander round his workshop. He has abandoned the notion of inspiration. The poet is no longer, as he was in William Blake, God's secretary taking down rapidly from dictation. The painter's sketchbook, the writer's notebook, is there for us to see, and just as there are museums which collect the drawings of old masters, so there is a special library (in America of course) of manuscript drafts and "Work in Progress" of modern poetry. Only three years ago appeared that great revelation *The Notebooks of Henry James,* and six years ago the first draft of Joyce's *Portrait of the Artist*. We are beginning to know how a great work comes into being. We are delighted to be admitted to the process as well as to enjoy the achievement. It was Dorothy Richardson who said that she was interested in a novel not for what it said, but for the picture it gave of the author. The artist is himself his chief creation. The only real biography of Shakespeare we have is the sum total of his plays and his poems.

For a long while, under the domination of the realist

approach, we demanded objectivity and aloofness from the novelist. We were horrified when he abruptly intruded himself, as Thackeray did in *Vanity Fair*, and nothing was more maddening than to be addressed as "Dear Reader." We were pulled sharply out of our daydreams, we were recalled violently from our holiday, we hadn't escaped after all. Nowadays one of the most noteworthy things in fiction is the way in which the novelist not only intrudes, but makes his intrusion an integral part of the work of art he is presenting. The conscious novelist is himself not only a part of the novel, but often the most important part.

The classic example among modern novels is André Gide's *The Counterfeiters* (*Les Faux Monnayeurs*) published in 1925. It is a novel about a novelist who is writing a novel. While he is writing this novel, the novelist, (that is, the one in the novel), keeps a diary recording the progress of his task. To complicate matters still further, André Gide himself kept a real diary while he was writing his novel about a novelist who keeps a diary while he is writing a novel. In the wake of this book, Aldous Huxley in 1928 wrote his *Point Counter Point*, whose very title reveals an attitude towards the structure of fiction. He uses the same device. Several of the chapters are headed "From Philip Quarles' Notebook." It is a fivefold complication. There is the novelist commenting in his notebook on the nature of fiction. There is the title of the book, *Point Counter Point*, labelling the structure and the method. There is the motto from Fulke Greville underlining the idea of counterpoint:

> Oh, wearisome condition of humanity,
> Born under one law, to another bound,
> Vainly begot and yet forbidden vanity,
> Created sick, commanded to be sound,
>   What meaneth nature by these diverse laws,
>   Passion and reason, self-division's cause?

In the foreground of the novel there is the story itself, but even the deployment of that is an object lesson in the discontinuity of time, and finally the characters, who are presented with diabolical clarity, are themselves vehicles, in accordance with Mr. Huxley's theory, of the ideas which form the counterpoint of the book. It is a "novel of ideas."

That is the heading of one of the paragraphs in Philip Quarles' notebook:

> "Novel of ideas. The character of each personage must be implied, as far as possible, in the ideas of which he is the mouthpiece. In so far as theories are rationalizations of sentiments, instincts, dispositions of soul, this is feasible. The chief defect of the novel of ideas is that you must write about people who have ideas to express—which excludes all but about ·01 per cent of the human race. Hence the real, the congenital novelists don't write such books. But then I never pretended to be a congenital novelist."

The next theme is not stated explicitly until nearly the end of the book, when Mark Rampion puts forward his theory. Men are always moving away from the "central norm" of humanity, "And all perverted in the same way —by trying to be non-human. Non-humanly religious, non-humanly moral, non-humanly intellectual and scientific, non-humanly specialized and efficient, non-humanly the business man, non-humanly avaricious and property-loving, non-humanly lascivious and Don Juanesque, non-humanly the conscious individual even in love. All perverts. Perverted towards goodness or badness, towards spirit or flesh. The world's an asylum of perverts." That temporarily, and more than temporarily, is Aldous Huxley's philosophy. To make it worse, most of the characters in the book are real people. Mark Rampion is D. H. Lawrence, and when Lawrence saw the book he pounced unerringly on this character. "Your Mark Rampion," he said "is the most boring character in the book—a gas-bag."

In my first lecture I quoted Galsworthy on Lawrence. You should in fairness read Lawrence on Galsworthy. It appears in one of Mr. Rickword's volumes of *Scrutinies*. Let me complete the chain by quoting Lawrence on Aldous Huxley. He lived long enough to read *Point Counter Point* and this is what he said:

"I have read *Point Counter Point* with a heart sinking through my boot-soles and a rising admiration.

"I do think that art has to reveal the palpitating moment or the state of man as it is. And I think you do that, terribly. But what a moment! and what a state! if you can only palpitate to murder, suicide and rape, in their various degrees—and you state plainly that it is so—however are we going to live through the days? Preparing still another murder, suicide, and rape? But it becomes of a phantasmal boredom and produces ultimately inertia, inertia, inertia and finally atrophy of the feelings. Till, I suppose, comes a final super-war, and murder, suicide, rape sweeps away the vast bulk of mankind."

The other half of the book is *Eyeless in Gaza*, using Milton's earlier struggle in *Samson Agonistes* as a temporary myth. There the discontinuity of time is more boldly used. There he gives more and more reverie of ideas. The stream of consciousness, of impressions and feelings, has become the stream of thought.

Where have we seen this before? Not merely in Gide's *Counterfeiters* and Wells's novels of discussion, to both of which Huxley is indebted, but in the grand old master Laurence Sterne's *Tristram Shandy*. In *The Life and Opinions of Tristram Shandy* there are, of course, no novelist's notebooks; it is all dispersed and distributed comment. But, above all, the discontinuity of time is there, superbly handled. You remember the startling and lovely sentence, "a cow broke in *to-morrow morning* to my Uncle Toby's fortifications." Then it seemed a joke. Now time is part of the serious problem of our day.

Between the two halves of Huxley's book, between *Point Counter Point* in 1928 and *Eyeless in Gaza* in 1936, came a very remarkable book, one of the greatest achievements of the twentieth century, Hermann Broch's *The Sleepwalkers*, to which I have already referred in another connection. It appeared in 1932 in a masterly translation by Edwin and Willa Muir, to whom this generation owes as big a debt for giving us this and Kafka and Ludwig Renns's *War* and other German books, as an earlier generation did to Mrs. Constance Garnett for her gifts from the Russian. I do not know specifically how much Aldous Huxley owes to Hermann Broch, but I do know that he has called it "a work of first-rate importance." The link between them is that both represent the novelist as encyclopædist, the novelist as polymath, as "polyhistor." Huxley's novels are full of dissertations woven into the narrative or bluntly stuck into the narrative, dissertations on history, on sociology, on music, on art, on philosophy, on Pavlov's conditioned reflexes, on everything under the sun. The difference between them is that where Huxley presents a montage of comment, Hermann Broch gives a philosophy of history. Where Aldous Huxley is knowing and smart and witty about his knowledge, Broch is serious and wise. He is not one of the permanently bright young things of the creative world.

In *The Sleepwalkers* the web of life is presented in all its intricacy, and at the same time explained and interpreted. The characters are brilliantly rendered, yet every single sentence, by its texture and its form, is an explanation. In the third section there is an overall explanation, the long treatise on "The Disintegration of Values," which marches relentlessly but intermittently as the most important of the many narrative elements interwoven into this gigantic tapestry of the march of man, the march of mind and the march of time. I can't help thinking of Griffith's film *Intolerance*, which has the same virtuosity in managing its four-in-hand themes to an intellectual as well as a pictorial conclusion. But *The Sleepwalkers* is like a film in which the captions are not only the most important part, but an integral part of the montage structure. I can't help comparing it also with those startling and stimulating novels, John Dos Passos's *Manhattan Transfer* and *The 42nd Parallel* with their cinematic devices, also, like *The Sleepwalkers*, under the strong influence of James Joyce. There, though the interwoven narrative is similar, it does not carry implicitly and punctiliously a philosophy of history, but only a picture of a teeming social world. It belongs rather to those metaphor novels of which I have previously spoken. "Life is like a journey." "Life is like a journey in a railway train." Here in *Manhattan Transfer* the metaphor—or simile if you prefer it—is "Life is like a railway junction." In *The Sleepwalkers* the age is conscious of itself and explains itself.

In Hermann Broch's *Death of Vergil*, another of the great books of the century, the parable is vaster. Its theme is "Literature at the end of a cultural epoch." He was asked to talk on this theme for the Vienna radio, but offered instead to present the same topic in the form of a short story. Out of those twenty pages grew this giant book set in the first century before Christ, a time of civil war and dictatorship and the dying away of the old religious forms. It presents the night and the day before the death of Vergil, who has resolved to destroy all his works, and the reasons for withdrawing that resolve. Vergil is seen, as the Middle Ages saw him, as the prophet of Christianity. Broch has written another novel, shortly to be published, whose theme is the analysis of mass hysteria, the psychosis from which the world has only recently and only partially been freed. Although his themes are chaos, disintegration and hysteria, Mr. Broch is almost the only optimist among all the great writers of this century.

In a world hurtling to its doom, as so many people seem to think it is, it is not surprising that the most natural preoccupation of that world should be—time. Time, as Mr. Graham Greene has called it, "that dark backward and abysm that is the novelist's abiding problem." In this twentieth century, which may be the last of centuries for man, we are obsessed with time. Philosophers analyse it, scientists abolish it, mathematicians transform it, and men of letters have it on the brain. The novels great and small—Proust's *In Search of Lost Time*, Aldous Huxley's *Time must have a Stop: Faster, Faster*: faster than sound, faster than light, time accelerated, time retarded, time and space. Our ears are dinned with it, in a thousand forms and disguises: time as duration, time as doom, "Time and Western Man," The March of Time, Time for Living, time for loving. Our favourite poems of the seventeenth century are Donne's *Ecstasy*, where time stands still, and Marvell's *Coy Mistress*, where time is slowed down and speeded up.

> Had we but world enough, and time,
> This coyness, Lady, were no crime.

· · · · ·

I would
Love you ten years before the Flood,
And you should, if you please, refuse
Till the conversion of the Jews.

. . . . .

An hundred years should go to praise
Thine eyes and on thy forehead gaze:
Two hundred to adore each breast,
But thirty thousand to the rest.

. . . . .

Nor would I love at lower rate.

But at my back I always hear
Time's winged chariot hurrying near;
And yonder all before us lie
Deserts of vast eternity.

And in this *Waste Land* of ours and Mr. Eliot's comes the
ominous cry, "Hurry up, please; it's time," "Hurry up,
please; it's time." In the great dramas of Sophocles and
Ibsen, in *Œdipus Rex* and *Rosmersholm*, time marches
forwards and backwards simultaneously. In Proust time
is elastic, it moves at different speeds, it is, as Proust
himself says, a fourth dimension. Time can be retarded,
it can be accelerated, and, as in the cinema, it can be
artificially constructed. It is curious how often the image
of the cinema has been evoked for the stream of consciousness and the problem of time, from Bergson onwards.

I have already spoken of the discontinuity of time in

Aldous Huxley. The most powerful instance of the interweaving of time and space that I know is in Jules Romains' *Men of Good Will*. When I spoke of the city as a symbol of our transitional and disintegrating age, I mentioned Joyce's Dublin and Canetti's Vienna and Döblin's Berlin, but I forgot two more familiar cities— Paris and New York. Fancy forgetting Paris and New York! Jules Romains' Paris and John Dos Passos's New York. Jules Romains had to create the city in which his unanimist philosophy was to manœuvre, and in the First Book, called "The 6th of October 1908" there is a chapter which is headed, "Introducing Paris at Five O'clock in the Evening," in which while eleven express trains are rushing towards Paris at seventy-five miles an hour, Paris is being built up from its history, its topographical growth, and its mass movements of people—space and time simultaneously. It has all the rushing excitement of Lumière's plain narrative film of the railway train at the first public film show in 1895, or of Hans Ruttmann's montage film *The Symphony of Berlin* more recently. Proust gives the credit to Flaubert for this modern innovation in the novel of the exact control over the passing of time, its contraction and expansion. But for most of us the source is once again Dostoevsky, in *The Idiot*, when he discusses the relation of time to a man condemned to death. "Just that instant, when you place your head on the block and hear the iron grate over your head, then that quarter of a second is the most awful of all." If by any chance you've missed it, I would urge you to read Horace McCoy's *tour de force, They*

Shoot Horses, Don't They?, in which the whole flash-
back of the story occurs in the pauses between the words
of the death sentence.

"Who doth Time gallop withal": asked Shakespeare,
"with a thief to the gallows; for though he go as softly
as foot can fall he thinks himself too soon there."

You know that moment in a film when the movement
is completely arrested, and for some special purpose of the
director, or sometimes only as a joke, the still picture
remains stationary on the screen. Motion is arrested.
Time stands still. I know nothing in modern writing
which quite achieves this, but there is an ancient specimen
which is hardly known, and which I have treasured since
I first came across it a quarter of a century ago. It is in
among the Apocryphal Gospels, in the Book of James.
St. Joseph has gone for a midwife for Mary, and while
he is seeking her the miracle of the birth of Jesus occurs.
There is no description of it, but in one paragraph, just
the expanded metaphor, "Time stood still," not stated,
but exemplified:

"Now I Joseph was walking, and I walked not. And
I looked up to the air and saw the air in amazement.
And I looked up unto the pole of the heaven and saw
it standing still, and the fowls of the heaven without
motion. And I looked upon the earth and saw a dish
set, and workmen lying by it, and their hands were in
the dish: and they that were chewing chewed not, and
they that were lifting the food lifted it not, and they
that put it to their mouth put it not thereto, but the
faces of all of them were looking upward. And behold

there were sheep being driven, and they went not forward but stood still; and the shepherd lifted his hand to smite them with his staff, and his hand remained up. And I looked upon the stream of the river and saw the mouths of the kids upon the water and they drank not. And of a sudden all things moved onward in their course."

Before I leave this theme, of time captured and recaptured, of time ordered and chaos conquered, I want to mention two English experiments, one vast and one small and modest. The first is Stephen Hudson's saga of "Richard Kurt," reprinted recently under the title of *A True Story*. It is one of the most intricate structural experiments of the century. In its present form it tells the story of a man, in chronological order, from his early childhood, through a tragic first marriage to a happy second one, in which a new personality is liberated. Not a very unusual story, but as it was originally written it was very far from being usual. It began with *Richard Kurt*, a deceptively simple story of a rich man idling life away on an Italian lake, building gardens and escaping from his worthless wife into a romantic adventure. The second volume, *Elinor Colhouse*, flashes back to America to the courtship and capture of Richard by his first wife. A searchlight has flooded the antecedents of the first novel, time has moved back, and clarification has moved forward. The third novel, *Prince Hempseed*, gives the growth of the young man who is to become the Richard Kurt of the first and second books, two different Richards, linked only by time, giving his growth from the age of five to eighteen in flashes (clearly inspired by Joyce's *Portrait of the Artist*) in prose minutely adjusted to the sensibility of each successive year of growth. These are tiny cross-sections, each a slice, not of life, but of time. The fourth novel is called *Tony* and is the death-bed monologue of the scapegrace brother of Richard, in which Tony is created, and Richard illuminated obliquely. Time shifts again, and is, as it were, sprinkled over the life of the hero like salt enriching the savour of his story. Then follows *Myrtle*, a number of scenes building up the second wife through the eyes of those who have admired and loved her, and also through the eyes of Richard Kurt himself, and in *Richard, Myrtle and I* there emerges a new artist-personality in Richard which is to become the person capable of writing this saga. These six volumes were published between 1919 and 1926, and there followed a long pause until 1937 when there appeared what is perhaps the most perfect of all the individual volumes—*The Other Side*, a brilliant evocation of America in the 1880's as it was when Richard as a youth first meets Elinor Colhouse.

Between 1926 and 1937 Hudson had translated Proust's last volume, *Time Regained*, in which the vast edifice of the search for time past is explained and justified. All that goes into *The Other Side* and gives it the durability it has. "It was that notion of the embodiment of time," says Proust, "the inseparableness from us of the past that I now had the intention of bringing strongly into relief in my work. And it is because they thus contain the past that human bodies can so much hurt those who love them, because they contain so many memories, so many joys and desires effaced within them. . . . I had a feeling of immense fatigue when I realized that all this span of time had not only been lived, thought, secreted by me uninterruptedly, that it was my life, that it was myself . . . that I was poised on its dizzy summit, that I could not move without taking it with me." All this in Hudson is lost and destroyed if the work is rearranged in chronological order. It is worth following the exact footsteps of the author in this English search for time past. I think that Stephen Hudson will grow in stature when this half-century is seen in the perspective of retrospect, for he was in touch with the age in an unusual number of ways. He translated that essay by Hermann Hesse, *In Sight of Chaos*, which I have already mentioned. He was the only English friend of Proust; he translated *Time Regained*. He knew James Joyce, and it was he who gave the famous party at which Proust and Joyce met, even if they could not communicate, and Hermann Broch's *Death of Vergil* is dedicated to the memory of Stephen Hudson.

The other experiment is by a young man, and appeared only three years ago. It is Philip Toynbee's *Tea with Mrs. Goodman*, and it has been attacked more viciously than any other important book I know. I can't say that it will always remain important on the public level, but I do think it is the kind of book which will be rediscovered by generation after generation as a private treasure and may even become a symbol of this age's attempt to pin down the fluttering butterfly of time.

I

Stephen Hudson's work is prose full of prose precision. Philip Toynbee's is prose full of the evocative precision of poetry. Not only is time called back, but it returns again and again in order to have its lineaments traced more and more accurately, the gaps filled in, the stresses balanced and the final outlines clarified. Just as Joyce becomes clearer and clearer as his methods are diluted into the ordinary stream of fiction, so when we are more accustomed to deal with myths, will this pattern become clearer.

Each of the seven narrators retraces the time of the tea party, or such part of it as he or she covers, and out of it by reinforcements of simultaneous moments of time the whole unity is built up. There is a before and after and a set of mythological and anthropological overtones. For the enlightenment of the reader there is a plan of the procedure, rather more puzzling than the procedure itself. The method is rather like that of a Japanese colour-print, where each colour is laid on with a separate block, which prints only those parts that are to receive the colour, and each block, whether of colour or narration, is either meaningless or cryptic when examined alone. Out of the superimposition of the several blocks the final picture is made clear, but, unlike the Japanese print, the key block in black outline is missing, the time-synthesis must be made in the imagination. It is not just a trick, something is achieved which could be done by no other method. It is not for all tastes. It makes tremendous demands. Like all the books I have mentioned, it is not one of those books which Mr. Michael Sadleir calls

" 'wholesome' novels of genial British make-believe." You must take your time over it. It must sink slowly in, like poetry.

I haven't said anything about Joyce's treatment of one day of time in *Ulysses* or Virginia Woolf's inspired imitation of it in *Mrs. Dalloway*, or her experiments in *To the Lighthouse* and *The Waves* and the *Years* or the Bloomsbury joke which became serious in *Orlando*, or the history of England in her last novel, *Between the Acts*, or of Joyce's treatment of eternity in *Finnegans Wake*. Jung said that *Ulysses* has neither beginning nor end, and that it can be read either backwards or forwards. This is not true of *Ulysses*, but it is almost true of *Finnegans Wake*, which begins in the middle of a sentence and ends in the middle of the same sentence, so that the reading can go on and on, round and round, to all eternity. But I hope I have said enough to suggest that the problem of time has some importance in the twentieth century.

The greater the chaos, it has been said, the greater the order which results from subduing it. A thousand paths must be used to approach it: allegory and analogy, the philosophy of history, the personally conducted tour through it, the neat, tidy packeted sample of chaos, or the help of the cinema with its flux and montage, its power of darting, its devices of narration, its controlled ecstasies of chase and climax, its camera angles and simultaneity, its wedding of music and motion. There is something of it in *The Waves*, and in *Tea with Mrs. Goodman*, in the agricultural show in *Madame Bovary* or the simultaneities in Pérez de Ayala's *Tiger Juan*, or Dos

Passos's *Manhattan Transfer*, or *Wuthering Heights* even.
There is something of it in the brackets of time in Virginia
Woolf, something even in that blinding flash in Mr.
Aldous Huxley's *Ape and Essence*: " 'Saturation bombing,' what a deliciously juicy phrase," something in the
devastating bracket in Ernest Hemingway's new book
which pins down half the agony of man. You remember
how the book is built. It opens with a duck-shooting
party during which a Venetian boatman is surly. This
surliness stretches and looms over the whole length of the
book, until its end, when another duck-shooting party
takes place. The boatman is still surly. And if by any
chance we had forgotten it, we are forcibly reminded.
The Colonel asks his host why the boatman is surly.
"It was the old battle-jacket. You see, he was a bit over-
liberated. When the Moroccans came through here they
raped both his wife and his daughter." Swift could not
have poised it better: "The most pernicious race of little
odious vermin that nature ever suffered to crawl upon the
surface of the earth."

It is good to think that the English novel is not isolated,
either in time or in space.

V

T. S. ELIOT AND
POETIC DRAMA

T. S. Eliot and Poetic Drama

SO far I have been speaking mainly of prose, and above all of prose fiction, as the ever-encroaching form of modern literature. And most of what I have been discussing has lain in the past. The glories lie behind; the summit of the 'twenties, the brilliant flashes of the 'thirties, and the decadence and bewilderment in the 'forties. These encroachments of prose have been upon the most ancient kind of literature—poetry. But amid all this reign of prose, slowly and steadily poetry has crept back again. It has to some extent, as we have seen, invaded the novel, but the field in which it has made its greatest conquests is the field of drama, and it is not so much a conquest as a re-conquest. We are witnessing the re-conquest of the novel by poetry, and the re-conquest of the drama by poetry, for both of these forms were originally in poetry. That has never really been lost sight of by the creators themselves. You remember how Fielding defined the novel, when it had at last become prose fiction. He called it "the comic-epic-poem *in prose.*" The poets have never acquiesced in the view that drama has been taken irrevocably out of their hands. For 300 years there has been a rearguard action, and a permanent resistance movement, with the usual squabbles within the party. Should it be in blank verse like the Elizabethan drama, or should it be in couplets like the new French masterpieces of the seventeenth century? And more recently, should it be rhetoric or plain colloquial speech? The two forms seem to be passing each other on the stairs—the novel on the way down, and the drama on the way up. At last there is hope. It is 300 years since there have been such signs of hope as there have been during the past twenty years, and that hope extends boldly into the future, for we are only just at the beginning.

We must preserve our perspective. A thousand years in the sight of the Lord are but as yesterday, we know, but nothing like the concentrated efflorescence of our great Elizabethan Age has ever been known. Greek drama covered a century or more, but the whole Elizabethan flourishing is exactly fifty years, the length of the half-century I have been trying to assess, from about 1590 to about 1640, from Marlowe and Kyd and Shakespeare to Webster and Ford and Beaumont and Fletcher; or, as John Davidson once wrote—

> From *Gorboduc* to *The Tempest* fifty years
> And nothing since.

We so far have had only from about 1930, and out of that time there has been a lull of ten years. I have tried to emphasize the fact that accompanying the march of literature there has been a constant enquiry into its meaning and processes, the age assessing itself, anxiously taking stock every five minutes, as it were, hoping to be able to report achievement and progress. So it has been in pure poetry, lyrical poetry, and so it has been in poetic drama. And the one name which stands out in both directions is that of Mr. T. S. Eliot. His *Sweeney Agonistes* began the new movement, and he has continued it to the marking-time of *The Cocktail Party*, and in between there has been the work of Mr. Auden, with or without his collaborator, Mr. Isherwood. Mr. Eliot is a critic, and as a critic who is also a creator he is incessantly and relentlessly concerned to discover precisely what his chosen form is after, its conditions, its needs, its difficulties and its aims. He has tried, if I may use the modern idiom, to pin-point the target. And this has been going on, not merely for the twenty years during which we have once more become aware of poetic drama as an important part of our mechanism for dealing with the present age, but for at least thirty years. In 1920 he wrote on *The Possibility of a Poetic Drama*, in 1928, in the margin of Dryden, a *Dialogue on Dramatic Poetry* and later, on *The Need for Poetic Drama*, on *The Future of Poetic Drama* and most recently on *The Aims of Poetic Drama*, exploring on the way, the drama of the Elizabethan renaissance, and Religious Drama ancient and modern.

Let me try to situate his strivings and his achievement in their historical perspective. When Mr. Eliot set out on his quest, the only persons who were seriously concerned with poetic drama were W. B. Yeats and Gordon Bottomley and Sturge Moore, but it was a muddled search, looking backward towards Shakespeare and national myths, with only one hopeful sign: the search for a people's language as a fit garment for a people's drama. That speech of the people was found in the Dublin Abbey Theatre, in the plays of J. M. Synge, and it turned out to be prose. The first real poetic drama of the century was poetic drama in prose. In 1916 came Ezra Pound and Fennollosa's book on the Japanese Noh plays, which changed the whole course of W. B. Yeats's enquiries towards symbolism, with musicians and dancers as part of the pattern. Yeats wrote an introduction to an edition of the Noh plays and Mr. Eliot was taken by Ezra Pound to a private performance of Yeats's play *The Hawk's Well*. It is interesting too that one of the earliest things Mr. Eliot wrote for *The Egoist* was a review of Ezra Pound's book and that in it he shows some of his earliest concern with dramatic problems. "The more symbolic drama is," he wrote, "the more we need the actual stage," and in the light of his play *The Family Reunion* twenty-two years later, it is not without significance that he is already concerned with the phantoms in the mind of Orestes. In 1919 and 1920 he concentrated on the Elizabethan dramatists, both in the study, and on the stage at the Phœnix Society, which did such valuable work between 1919 and 1925. The Phœnix Society reminded us that Shakespeare was not the only Elizabethan, and made poetic drama a living poetry to be listened to and not merely looked at on the page. It showed a hundred tasks and a hundred characters dealt with in flexible verse by a school of dramatists in close touch with their age. Mr. Eliot went on writing about Elizabethan drama, and the Renaissance struggles with blank verse, until at least 1934, the year of his first play *The Rock*.

When he came to write he was well prepared. As far back as 1911 he had combined the dramatic monologue of Browning and of Laforgue in *The Love Song of J. Alfred Prufrock*. The brooding figure of Agamemnon entered into *Sweeney Among the Nightingales.*:

> The nightingales are singing near
> The Convent of the Sacred Heart,
>
> And sang within the bloody wood
> When Agamemnon cried aloud,
> And let their liquid siftings fall
> To stain the stiff dishonoured shroud.

The nightingale's thicket enters once again into *The Family Reunion*. The new order begins officially in 1932 when *Sweeney Agonistes, an Aristophanic Melodrama* was published in volume form. We must be careful about dates, for they can be very misleading. If we notice that Mr. Auden's volume of *Poems* in 1930 contained a charade, *Paid on Both Sides*, and that his book *The Orators* appeared in 1932, we might be led to suppose that Mr. Auden's dramatic work developed in complete independence of Mr. Eliot's, and that even *The Dance of Death* in 1933 appeared too soon for any real indebtedness. But *Sweeney Agonistes* had already been printed in *The Criterion* in October, 1926, and January, 1927, and had its discreet and growing influence during the intervening five years.

We must watch this rather closely; it is a very intricate business. It is as bad as *Œdipus Rex* or *Rosmersholm*: it all has to be unravelled backwards. I wish we knew as much about the Elizabethans, about the criss-cross of influences between Shakespeare and Beaumont and Fletcher, for instance, when the fashionable new romantic drama came along. I have more than a feeling that Shakespeare's contemporaries, not the public, of course, but his fellow dramatists, watched him as closely then as Mr. Eliot's contemporaries now weigh up his every phrase and every poetical or dramatic hint. One of these days I am going to try to straighten out Shakespeare's takings-in and givings-out, but at the moment my business is with Mr. Eliot.

In May and June, 1934, there was performed at Sadler's Wells a Pageant called *The Rock*, "The Book of Words" by T. S. Eliot. The year before there had been published, and in February of the same year as *The Rock* there had been performed, Mr. Sean O'Casey's play *Within the Gates*. In November, 1933, Messrs. Faber and Faber published Mr. Auden's *The Dance of Death*, a new kind of play for England. The opening statement by the announcer says: "We present to you this evening a picture of the decline of a class, of how its members dream of a new life, but secretly desire the old, for there is death inside them. We show you that death as a dancer," and the Chorus, behind a curtain, cries, "Our death." In April, 1934, there was performed at the Comédie des Champs Elysées in Paris M. Jean Cocteau's *The Infernal Machine*, a new version of Sophocles' *Œdipus Rex*, a poetic drama in prose. The end of the Prologue says: "Spectator, this machine, you see here wound up to the full, in such a way that the spring will slowly unwind the whole length of a human life, is one of the most perfect constructed by the infernal gods for the mathematical destruction of a mortal." This play was performed by the Stage Society in London in 1935.

The twin streams of Auden and Eliot moved on, in 1935 almost side by side. In 1935 there was Mr. Eliot's *Murder in the Cathedral*, first at Canterbury in the Chapter House, and then in London at the Mercury. Then, published in May, 1935, and performed in January, 1936, by the Group Theatre, there came *The Dog Beneath the Skin*, by W. H. Auden and Christopher Isherwood. And here, what appears to be a parallel stream resolves itself into a dichotomy of the age. Where Mr. Eliot concludes his plays with some piece or parallel of the Christian liturgy, Mr. Auden plunges into the Communist manifesto. *Murder in The Cathedral* ends with a chorus of prayer:

> We acknowledge our trespass, our weakness, our fault; we acknowledge
> That the sin of the world is upon our heads; that the blood of the martyrs and the agony of the saints
> Is upon our heads.
> Lord, have mercy upon us.
> Christ, have mercy upon us.
> Lord, have mercy upon us.
> Blessed Thomas, pray for us.

In *The Dog Beneath the Skin*, the Chorus shouts one concluding line:

> To each his need: from each his power,

which is Karl Marx saying, in the margin of the German Workers' Party in 1875, "From each according to his ability, to each according to his needs." Earlier still, at the end of Mr. Eliot's *The Rock*, the Archbishop blesses the people, but in Mr. Auden's *Dance of Death*, the God out of the Machine is Karl Marx again who says, "The instruments of production have been too much for him. He is liquidated."

In 1936 came Auden and Isherwood's *The Ascent of F.6*, still powerful and dramatic in its effect after fourteen years, as the recent broadcast performance proved, and in 1938 their last play, *On the Frontier*, with its song to the tune of "Mademoiselle from Armentières," and then, in 1939, Mr. Eliot's *The Family Reunion*, a modern play on the theme of Orestes and the Eumenides. After that there is a lull, except for some interesting younger dramatists like Mr. Ronald Duncan with his *This Way to the Tomb*, and Mrs. Anne Ridler with *The Shadow Factory* and *Cain* and her recent volume of *Henry Bly and other Plays*. After the lull Mr. Auden's *The Age of Anxiety* comes into the picture in 1948 (though not strictly a play, it fits in, perhaps, like Milton's *Comus*), and Mr. Eliot's *The Cocktail Party* is still part of the present climate of poetical and dramatic opinion. Mr. Christopher Fry represents a different direction.

What is it that marks these plays off from the commercial drama, and from previous plays in verse or even in prose, and forces us to classify them as poetic drama? There is, first, their mixture of high seriousness in poetry and human colloquial speech, both in prose and verse.

There is the tone of liveliness and intensity. There is the
action on more than one level, the perpetual parable or
allegory, and there is, finally, the startling variety of
elements derived from every conceivable theatrical
activity past and present. In short, there is a wider
theatrical equipment harnessed to a deeper poetical
purpose. It is not intended to be read in the study, as so
many earlier verse plays have been, it is meant to be
living theatre for the people. And that is why so many
popular forms of proved effect upon an audience are
utilized or incorporated in it. Modern drama was born
when the congregation in a church became an audience
outside it. The most ancient and most powerful dramatic
effect is that of liturgical ritual upon a group of spectators
or participants. The modern poetic drama, whether its
purpose is religious or political, wishes to turn the
audience into participants sharing a common myth while
still remaining spectators. Without that common myth,
whether it be the myth behind ancient Greek tragedy or
comedy, or the miracle plays and morality plays of
medieval Christianity, or even the modern music-hall,
nothing can be built up. The new poetic dramatists wish
to see and to work for an audience as united and as eager,
and as appreciative of fine points of technique, as those
attending the Dionysian Festivals or the modern Cup
Final, or the bullfight or the baseball game.

Mr. Eliot called *The Rock* a "revue," and we know
what a revue is. A revue is something put on by Mr.
André Charlot or Sir Charles Cochran, something by
Mr. Noel Coward, like *This Year of Grace. Cavalcade* is

a revue really. In *The Dog Beneath the Skin* the initial
mood is fixed by the poetical chorus, with its contemporary images cunningly and powerfully deployed—as
powerfully as the comparable images in Greek tragedy
or medieval miracle plays.

Hiker with sunburn blisters on your office pallor,
Cross-country champion with corks in your hands,
When you have eaten your sandwich, your salt and your
    apple,
When you have begged your glass of milk from the ill-
    kept farm,
What is it you see?

I see barns falling, fences broken,
Pasture not ploughland, weeds not wheat.
The great houses remain but only half are inhabited,
Dusty the gunrooms and the stable clocks stationary.

Those who sang in the inns at evening have departed;
    they saw their hope in another country.

Then the play opens in a setting of musical comedy, with
comedy chorus rhythms, there are Noel Coward revue
lyrics, Cole Porter songs. There is a scene in a lunatic
asylum, another in a hospital operating theatre, a cabaret
in the Grand Nineveh Hotel, with a devastating chorus
singing:
              Neat girls, sweet girls,
              Gym girls, slim girls,
              Meek girls, technique girls,
              Pat girls, com-up-to-my-flat girls, we
                  Hope to see you again!

The macabre scene in the cabaret where Destructive Desmond dressed as a schoolboy slashes to pieces a guaranteed genuine Rembrandt painting is a cruel cold and deadly perversion of the Marx Brothers, without any of their warmth and kindness. There is jazz and blue and a Vicar's sermon, and after the *Walpurgisnacht* the poetical Chorus sums up:

So, under the local images your blood has conjured,
We show you man caught in the trap of his terror,
    destroying himself.

.   .   .   .   .

Do not speak of a change of heart, meaning five hundred
    a year and a room of one's own,
As if that were all that is necessary.

.   .   .   .   .

Beware of yourself:
Have you not heard your own heart whisper: "I am the
    nicest person in this room"?
Asking to be introduced to someone 'real': someone un-
    like all those people over there?

.   .   .   .   .

Repent. . . . Unite. . . . Act.

I have never known an audience or a congregation so united as it was at the Group Theatre performance in January, 1936, in one convulsive shudder of guilt at those words, "I am the nicest person in this room." With such common myths does the modern poetic dramatist begin to build his edifice.

K

As far back as 1921, long before he had attempted anything dramatic, Mr. Eliot sought another foundation for
dramatic myth, in the English music-hall. He wrote that
"Little Tich, George Robey, Nellie Wallace, Marie
Lloyd, George Mozart, Lupino Lane . . . provide fragments of a possible English myth. They effect the Comic
Purgation." "The modern dramatist, and probably the
modern audience, is terrified of the myth. The myth is
imagination and it is also criticism, and the two are one."
Time and time again he came back to this theme, of the
music-hall as a fundamental tributary of drama. On the
death of Marie Lloyd in 1923 he wrote: "The working
man who went to the music-hall and saw Marie Lloyd
and joined in the chorus was himself performing part of
the act; he was engaged in that collaboration of the
audience with the artist which is necessary in all art and
most obviously in dramatic art." In 1928, in his *Dialogue
on Dramatic Poetry*, he was probing deeper into the nature
and sources of drama. There was the ballet, the Russian
Ballet: "Here seemed to be everything that we wanted
in drama, except the poetry. . . . If there is a future for
drama, and particularly for poetic drama, will it not be
in the direction indicated by the ballet?" There is also the
liturgy: "Drama springs from religious liturgy, and it
cannot afford to depart far from religious liturgy. . . ."
And, finally, one of the speakers in the dialogue comes
back to the music-hall and popular drama. "Take the
humour of our great English comedian, Ernie Lotinga."
He says, "It is (if you like) bawdy. But such bawdiness is
a tribute to, an acknowledgment of conventional British

morality. I am a member of the Labour Party. I believe
in the King and the Islington Empire. I do not believe in
the plutocratic St. Moritzers for whom our popular
dramatists cater. But what I was saying is that our
suburban drama is morally sound, and out of such
soundness poetry may come."

By then Mr. Eliot had written his first dramatic piece,
Sweeney Agonistes, an Aristophanic Melodrama. He had
had his Comic Purgation, and was feeling good. So the
tone of his "Dialogue" seems to imply. Whether this
purgation came directly from Aristophanes or indirectly
from Ernie Lotinga, who is not only bawdy, but a direct
descendant of the phallic comedy of Greece and Rome,
I do not know. This I do know, that if I have done
nothing else for literature, I did at least take Mr. Eliot to
see Mr. Ernie Lotinga at the Islington Empire.

The phallic, the Dionysian, the Aristophanic! This
modern poetic drama seems to have pretty deep roots.
In *Sweeney Agonistes*, which underwent the test of
performance by the Group Theatre in January, 1933,
Mr. Eliot, it seems to me, was trying to see whether
tragic feelings could be expressed, not through the
obvious medium of tragedy, but through the medium of
farce. The performance, which I remember very well,
and which I believe somewhat puzzled Mr. Eliot, while
preserving the farce, completely blurred the tragedy
which is perfectly clear in the text.

Long before he wrote *The Rock*, Mr. Eliot seems to
have delved pretty deeply into the ritual origins of
ancient drama, and in *The Rock* this ritual element, this

liturgical element, is strongly present, in the choruses which are all that he prefers to retain of the Pageant. It was written to somebody else's scenario and apart from the choruses was a shedding, a getting out of his system of most of the revue element and the music-hall element that remained longer in Mr. Auden, because it fitted in better with the political direction the Auden type of play was serving. Mr. Eliot's new direction lay primarily in the experiments in liturgical writing of the choruses, the religious explorations which were to become increasingly urgent in the later plays.

Murder in the Cathedral is a transitional play, whose chief importance again lies in the choruses, the beautiful choruses of the women of Canterbury.

Since golden October declined into sombre November
And the apples were gathered and stored, and the land
    became brown sharp points of death in a waste of
    water and mud,
The New Year waits, breathes, waits, whispers in
    darkness.
While the labourer kicks off a muddy boot and stretches
    his hand to the fire,
The New Year waits, destiny waits for the coming.

There is still a certain crudity in the shock tactics of the murderous knights, there is still too much topicality, but it was a great success, partly because of the theme, partly because of those same knights, and partly because of the title. What a box-office title! Hall Caine used to say that the secret of the best-seller was a judicious mixture of sex and religion. Here was a mixture even closer to both the interests of the time, crime and religion. There has only been one other title comparable in topicality—*Love on the Dole*. I am happy to learn that *Murder in the Cathedral* was not Mr. Eliot's choice; his original title was "Fear in the Way," and under such a title it would have fallen dead flat, I am sure. The selling title was suggested, I believe, by Mrs. Martin Browne, and under that title it became a popular success.

In *Sweeney Agonistes* one of the mottoes was from Æschylus; Orestes' exit-line at the end of *The Libation Bearers*, about the Furies. "You don't see them, you don't —but *I* see them: they are hunting me down." *The Family Reunion* takes this for its whole theme. At one time Mr. Eliot even intended to call the play "Follow the Furies." Almost as soon as he arrives in the house, Harry Monchensey, who is Orestes, uses the same words, but with a more urgent rhythm:

> Look there!
> Can't you see them? *You* don't see them, but I see them,
> And they see me.

The play is, like the Agamemnon trilogy, the story of a curse on the generations of a family, a curse on a house, a sin that is twice repeated, or the shadow of a sin, the death of Harry's wife, whether he really killed her or merely wished to kill her, and the murderous thought of Harry's father, who wanted to kill Harry's mother. It is linked with Henry James's story about a house, *The*

Jolly Corner, and Yeats's play about a house, *Purgatory*.
Like all plays of this kind, plays of ancient myth in a modern setting and with modern relevance, it is written on more than one plane, and when the immediate plane is nearest, it comes as a shock, just as the knights do in *Murder in the Cathedral* when they slip out of the play and up to the footlights like a music-hall turn. The shock here, in *The Family Reunion*, is the double irony, the dramatic irony of the figure of Sergeant Winchell, the policeman. Mr. Eliot in those days was a great amateur of the detective story—he even laid down a set of Aristotelian canons for its literary conduct, and the red-herring shock comes when the police sergeant enquires after the dead Lady Monchensey, but this *is* only a red herring. As Mr. Eliot writes in the play:

> What we have written is not a story of detection,
> Of crime and punishment, but of sin and expiation.

I think that here Mr. Eliot, who was a close student of Dostoevsky, is pointing out that the English title, *Crime and Punishment*, does not represent the theme of Dostoevsky's novel, and that *Sin and Expiation*, which comes out more clearly in the German title, *Schuld und Sühne*, is much closer. He has explained that "the Furies are *divine* instruments, not simple hell-hounds" and that they appear to Harry the second time as "divine messengers, to let him know clearly that the only way out is purgation and holiness," so that "Harry's career needs to be completed by an *Orestes* or an *Œdipus at Colonnus*." Is it possible that one day Mr. Eliot may be tempted to give us a complete modern trilogy on some modern agony?

There has been much difference of opinion about this play. I think *The Family Reunion* is the most successful and most profound, and most personally felt, of all his plays. But it has been objected that Harry's story is so much inferior to that of Orestes for dramatic purposes because "the hatred of a wife, though repeated in two generations, does not, as Eliot handles it, assume much more than private significance." This play is a tragic interlude with no trace of comedy, between *Sweeney Agonistes* and *The Cocktail Party*, between Aristophanic melodrama and a comedy of the drawing-room, so labelled. I think we can throw a little light on the problem from some remarks of Mr. Eliot hidden away in a short article on Shakespearean criticism in the Cambridge *Companion to Shakespeare Studies* five years before.

"To those who have experienced the full horror of life," he says, "tragedy is still inadequate. Sophocles felt more of it than he could express, when he wrote *Œdipus the King*; Shakespeare, when he wrote *Hamlet*; and Shakespeare had the advantage of being able to employ his grave-diggers. In the end, horror and laughter may be one—only when horror and laughter have become as horrible and laughable as they can be; and—whatever the conscious intention of the authors—you may laugh or shudder over *Œdipus* or *Hamlet* or *King Lear*—or both at once: then only do you perceive the aim of the comic and the tragic dramatist is the same: they are equally serious . . . there is potential comedy in Sophocles and potential tragedy in Aristophanes, and otherwise they would not be such good tragedians or comedians as they are." Perhaps this may throw some light also on *The Cocktail Party* and the puzzlement that many people feel about it.

The Cocktail Party, labelled "a comedy," is full of comedy, at least so the audience at the New Theatre seemed to think the day I was there, for it laughed frequently and uneasily whenever the actors rang their little bells. Audiences are strange things. They tell you quite a lot about the plays they are watching. The audience at an Ernie Lotinga show is the pure unaltered audience that has persisted through Greek comedy and mime and Roman comedy, frankly appreciative of the age-old phallic mimes, guffawing and doubled up in agony, never simpering, never smirking, never squeamish, never prurient or mock-modest. It is a people's audience, even a family audience. I remember very vividly the audience of *The Rock* at Sadler's Wells in 1934. It was the first time poetic drama had really come to the people. It was a simple and devout audience, a rapt and uncomprehending audience, moved by the liturgical patterns, laughing uneasily at the human lines as if they were afraid of being caught laughing in church.

> In this land
> There shall be one cigarette to two men,
> To two women one half pint of bitter
> Ale.

"A jester's a man what comes on and does the comic turn." "Oh, like George Robey!" It was an audience of

church workers, of mothers' outings, of shepherds and
their flocks, and a few "highbrows" like myself, who
were moved by the echoes of the Book of Nehemiah:

> In Shushan the palace, in the month Nisan,
> He served the wine to the king Artaxerxes,
>
> .　　　.　　　.　　　.
>
> And there, by the dragon's well, by the dung gate,
> By the fountain gate, by the king's pool,
> Jerusalem lay waste, consumed with fire;

highbrows who responded to topical Audenisms like:

> What does the world say, does the whole world stray
> 　　　in high-powered cars on a by-pass way?

or

> The wind shall say: "Here were decent godless people:
> Their only monument the asphalt road
> And a thousand lost golf balls."

or were flattered by recognizing a clerihew in the Christopher Wren scene "Ah . . . tell him I'm designing
St. Paul's." Liturgy, Bible, George Robey, Auden and
clerihew—there was something for everybody. But the
audience at *The Cocktail Party*, youthful, American,
willing, almost eager, resentful, puzzled, frustrated,
bewildered, disappointed, swindled, laughing and gig-
gling dutifully, manfully, bravely, hoping against hope,
shrugging the shoulders, getting everything except the
implications. It was very different in the days of Maeter-
linck. You remember the two dear old ladies who went
to see *The Blue Bird*, and when they came out, one of

them asked "Did you understand it, my dear?" "No, but I got the message!" The day I went, they did *not* get the message.

And yet that is the whole point of poetic drama—that it is written expressly to convey a message. But what do we mean by message, and how can a message be conveyed? There are two ways you can convey a message. You can hand it over obviously on a platter, or you can make the audience earn it—through poetry, that is. The manifest content is made clear to you, the latent content you have to earn. There is a third way: to make it easy by offering an obvious symbol as Ibsen does in *The Wild Duck* or *The Master Builders*. The first way is more suited to politics and that is the way Auden adopted, the second is more suited to religion, and that is the method Eliot adopted. Eliot is a traditional poet linked with almost everything, Auden is an ultra-modern poet concerned with anything which is of the age. Politics demands hysteria, and human beings treated as abstractions or statistics. That is the special approach of expressionist drama. You can see it in Mr. Elmer Rice's *The Adding Machine*, where the characters are Mr. and Mrs. Zero. Mr. and Mrs. One, Mr. and Mrs. Two, and so on, where the hysteria is built up, not on individual human feelings but on collective conditioned reflexes. Here is a sample. At the end of an argument a group of American men shout in unison.

ALL (*in unison*): That's it! Damn foreigners! Damn dagoes! Damn Catholics! Damn Sheenies! Damn

niggers! Jail 'em! Shoot 'em! Hang 'em! Lynch 'em!
Burn 'em! (*They all rise*)
    ALL (*singing in unison*): My country, 'tis of thee,
                                   Sweet land of liberty!

You can see the same hysteria, the same anonymity, in
Ernst Toller's *Masses and Men*, and in Georg Kaiser's
From Morn to Midnight, set in the places specially dedicated
to hysteria, the Salvation Army meeting, the Stock
Exchange, the Bicycle-Race Stadium. Mr. Isherwood
has said that the plays he wrote with Mr. Auden, especially *The Dog Beneath the Skin*, owe an enormous debt to
German Expressionism, to Bert Brecht's *Dreigroschenoper*
which we have seen as a film, and his *Stadt Mahagonny*.
"If the poetic drama has a rebirth in England," he wrote
in 1939, "and some people think it may—the movement
will be largely German in inspiration and origin." He
was speaking of the Auden contribution. Mr. Eliot's
contribution has different affiliations. Some of Eliot is
linked to Eugene O'Neill. The technique of soliloquy
in *The Family Reunion* goes back to O'Neill's *Strange
Interlude*. Sean O'Casey's *Within the Gates* acknowledges
a debt to O'Neill's *Mourning becomes Electra*, and there are
affinities, perhaps coincidental, between O'Casey's play
and Eliot's *The Rock*. O'Neill goes back to the Father of
Expressionism, Strindberg. In Stockholm the public
found O'Neill's difficult play *The Iceman Cometh* perfectly easy, because they had been brought up on Strindberg.

From Strindberg comes the whole of poetic drama in

Europe, from his *Dream Play*, his *Spook Sonata* and above all from his trilogy *The Road to Damascus*. *The Road to Damascus* is perhaps the greatest of modern dramatic achievements. It was written at the turn of the century, but was only published in English in 1939. It is a poetic drama of a special kind, and it is in prose. Its special kind is the same as *Everyman*, the Dutch morality play we have made our own ever since William Poel revived the medieval text, and it was presented again to the world through the agency of Max Reinhardt. Its characters, like *Everyman's*, are all abstractions or types: the Stranger, the Lady, the Beggar. When we produced the first part at the Stage Society in 1937, I devised a setting in the medieval morality manner, a series of mansions to be traversed in one direction and then back again to the first playing place where the action ended. Of course, it was not used, but it would have emphasised the morality structure of the play, the foreground reality, and the real play going on simultaneously on another plane, the process of *Œdipus Rex* and Cocteau's *The Infernal Machine* and T. S. Eliot's *The Family Reunion* and *The Cocktail Party*.

No poetical drama is simple. Every poetical play is constructed in overtones and implications. Mr. Eliot has said, in connection with *The Cocktail Party*, "I should not think very highly of any play of which I could gather the whole point after only seeing it once, and without having read it," and, if it is any consolation to those who feel puzzled and uncomfortable, "I should not like anyone seeing a play of mine to feel completely comfortable." History repeats itself, but in a different, more polite manner. When the Stage Society put on Tchehov's *The Cherry Orchard*, another poetic drama in prose, after the first act half the audience left, after the second act most of the remaining half, and by the end of the performance only the actors and the theatre staff remained in the building. The audience at *The Cocktail Party* has less courage, or better manners, or perhaps greater faith and hope in the poetic drama.

The excitement of English poetic drama for us is that it is in verse, and that it is English verse. Verse can do things which are beyond the capacity of prose. The vehicle of poetic drama is verse, its mechanism is imagery, its substance is myth and its binding structure is the musical pattern which gives an over-all unity to every tiny fragment of what is in the end a musical symphony. The poet's problems are many. Mr. Eliot points out that "a poet writes his ordinary poetry implicitly to be spoken by *himself*: he must write his dramatic poetry remembering that it is to be spoken by someone else. I find," he says, "that in my first draft of a play there are passages which seem to be first-rate, and they are likely to be the ones I have to remove . . . they are poetry, but they are my poetry and not that of my character who speaks them." In that shrewd observation lies the explanation of the failure of all those poets of the Romantic movement who tried their hand at poetic plays.

Where Mr. Eliot in his turn has succeeded is in the superb management of his choruses, and in the subtle employment of rhythms and tempos for purposes of poetic and dramatic climax. The verse, he says, in those parts of a play concerned with everyday affairs "should be unnoticeable—the audience should not be conscious of the difference from prose. The purpose of the verse should be to operate upon the auditor unconsciously, so that he shall think and feel in the rhythms imposed by the poet, without being aware of what these rhythms are doing. All the time, these rhythms should be *preparing* the ear of the audience for the moments of intensity, when the emotion of the character in the play may be supposed to lift him from his ordinary discourse, until the audience feels, not that the actors are speaking verse, but that the characters in the play have been lifted up into poetry." There are some hints of this in *The Cocktail Party*, and there would have been more perhaps if the actors had known how to speak the lines or the producer had been able to persuade them to do so. The summit of Mr. Eliot's achievement so far, for me at least, is in the two scenes of *The Family Reunion*, where the rhythms prepare the audience for the appearance of the Eumenides, where in fact the poetic rhythms create the Eumenides. The only adequate parallel I can think of is the scene in Shakespeare's *Julius Cæsar* in which the poetical rhythms prepare the appearance of the ghost of Cæsar in Brutus's tent.

The texture of poetic drama is verse, its substance is myth, that common possession which binds audience and dramatist together and provides a universe of discourse and of feeling out of which drama grows as naturally as a flower from the soil. I am sorry that I have no time to do more than mention the efforts which

French dramatists like Sartre and Camus and Anouilh are making to establish such a myth, either by harping on its necessity, or by reattaching the myths of classical tragedy to the modern predicament, as Sartre does in his splendid play *The Flies* or Anouilh in *Antigone*, or Jean Cocteau in *The Infernal Machine* and in *Orpheus*, and in his bravest of adventures, that startling and moving and beautiful film of *Orpheus* which has recently been shown in England.

Poetic drama is the literary form of the future. How can we jump on to the bandwagon? Mr. Eliot has devised a simple recipe which he sent in a lively letter to Mr. Ezra Pound. It was printed by Mr. Ronald Duncan with the permission of the writer and the recipient, and I am sure Mr. Eliot won't mind if I pass the formula on to you in his very words:

" 1. You got to keep the audience's attention all the time.

2. If you lose it you got to get it back QUICK.

3. Everything about plot and character and all else what Aristotle and others say is secondary to the forgoin.

4. But IF you can keep the bloody audience's attention engaged, then you can perform any monkey tricks you like when they ain't looking, and it's what you do behind the audience's back so to speak that makes your play IMMORTAL for a while.

If the audience gets its strip tease it will swallow the poetry.

5. If you write a play in verse, then the verse ought

to be a medium to look THROUGH and not a pretty decoration to look AT."

This is basic advice, but, speaking to the Poets' Theatre Guild, to the men who are hoping to produce the next generation of drama, Mr. Eliot does not promise any speedy or easy success. "We can only hope," he said, "that in the course of a generation or so, as a result of individual successes and failures—or, rather, as is likely, of partial successes and partial failures, by a kind of unconscious selection and rejection, a common medium will be hammered out. . . . What I hope we shall eventually get, is not one great dramatist, a solitary peak in a flat plain, but a cluster of dramatists. I regard our work to-day as that of the first generation only: my greatest hope is that we shall lay some foundations upon which others will come to build."

And I should like to conclude with something the Poet Laureate, Mr. John Masefield, said, very much to the point, forty years ago: "Our playwrights have all the powers except that power of exultation which comes from a delighted brooding on excessive, terrible things. That power is seldom granted to man; twice or thrice to a race, perhaps, not oftener. But it seems to me certain that every effort, however humble, towards the achieving of that power helps the genius of a race to obtain it, though the obtaining may be fifty years after the strivers are dead."

VI

THE VERDICT

The Verdict

THIS is the last lecture of this series, and I suppose I ought to devote it to explaining why I have not mentioned E. M. Forster, or such popular writers as J. B. Priestley, A. J. Cronin, Charles Morgan and Pearl Buck. E. M. Forster is a special case. I should have liked to discuss him at great length, in a more leisurely way, for he has earned great respect and has been a profound influence in some directions, but he doesn't fit into these sweeping and panoramic views I have been giving, and his last novel, *A Passage to India*, which was a startling book in its time, was published as far back as 1924. As for the others, who are only samples of the scores I have not mentioned, the principles and standards by which I have been judging should by now be apparent.

I have not even had time to deal with many writers for whom I have a great admiration and affection, or who would fit into a larger and more detailed survey. After all, I am trying to hint in six lectures at what would under normal academic conditions take about thirty-six to expound. I haven't therefore been able to deal with important historical or period figures like Gilbert Cannan or J. D. Beresford or Ford Madox Ford, or May Sinclair, or Ronald Firbank or Norman Douglas. I have not been able to express my admiration for the work

of Mr. William Plomer, for Miss Rebecca West's fine
novel *The Thinking Reed*, or Mr. Wyndham Lewis's
Tarr, which has just been reprinted, I believe. I have not
said more than a word about Bernard Shaw, who strides
the epoch like a colossus. There is no place in the pattern
for scores of individual achievements which, unfor-
tunately for my immediate purpose, do not point a
moral.

The thing that worries me most is that I have hardly
been able to say anything about literature, pure literature
—that is to say, lyrical poetry. Poetry, after all, is the life-
blood of literature, the living English tongue in its fullest
range of resources. The great novels I have spoken of are
international. They still retain 50 per cent. of their value
in translation, but nine-tenths of poetry disappears in
another tongue. I care infinitely more for poetry than I
do even for the novel and the drama, but it is not so easy
to talk about it, it does not fall so easily into historical
patterns, it needs such minute exposition, such dwelling
on details, on single images even. You can lecture on the
whole of Shakespeare in one hour, but it take two hours
to talk about one single speech. Because of this, and
because I have already spoken at some length in an earlier
series of talks on *The Background of Modern Poetry*, I can
only give a few hints of what has been achieved during
the past fifty years.

Something of the great changes can be seen in three
striking developments or transformations. W. B. Yeats,
the poet of "The Lake Isle of Innisfree," became the poet
of "Byzantium" and of the sonnet on "Leda and the

Swan." Miss Edith Sitwell, the poet of "The King of China's Daughter," has become the poet of "Still Falls the Rain" about the air-raids of 1940, and of "The Shadow of Cain" about the Atomic Bomb, and Mr. Eliot, the poet of *Prufrock* and *The Waste Land*, has become the poet of *Four Quartets*. It is some indication of the way in which English poetry has impinged on the outer world, that two of these poets, Yeats and Mr. T. S. Eliot, have been chosen as Nobel Prize-winners. From Thomas Hardy, the father of modern poetry, to whom poets like W. H. Auden have acknowledged a fundamental debt, and from Robert Bridges, the Poet Laureate to whom the Georgian poets unanimously dedicated their first volume, poetry has come a long way. The revolutionary change came with the Imagist poets, with T. E. Hulme, and F. S. Flint and Ezra Pound and Richard Aldington from 1908 onwards. The Imagist manifesto is well-known, but it was D. H. Lawrence, a late and temporary recruit, who expressed the essence of the movement. In January, 1916, he wrote in a letter to Catherine Carswell: "break the rhyme rather than the stony directness of speech. The essence of poetry with us in this age of stark and unlovely actualities is a stark directness, without a shadow of a lie, or a shadow of deflection anywhere. Everything can go, but this stark, bare, rocky directness of statement, this alone makes poetry to-day."

In the War of 1914–18 two potentially great English poets were sacrificed, Wilfred Owen and Isaac Rosenberg. Rosenberg appeared in Sir Edward Marsh's

Georgian Poetry, Owen in Miss Edith Sitwell's publication, *Wheels*. Each expressed the poetry and the pity of war, Owen in his "Strange Meeting," and Rosenberg in his "Dead Man's Dump." Isaac Rosenberg, had he lived, would have become a poetic dramatist of strange quality, and might perhaps have hastened the movement in poetic drama of which I have already spoken. His poems have just been reprinted, and now that the Group Theatre has resumed its activities, I should like to suggest that as it once performed Mr. Eliot's *Sweeney Agonistes* as an experiment, it might consider presenting as another experiment Mr. Christopher Fry's play *The Firstborn*, with Isaac Rosenberg's *Moses*, on the same subject, as a curtain-raiser. Rosenberg's dramatic verse is something to bite on. During the famine in Egypt:

> The satraps swore
> Their wives' bones hurt them when they lay abed
> That before were soft and plump. The people howled
> They'd boil the slaves three days to get their fat,
> Ending the famine. A haggard council held
> Decrees the two hind molars, those two staunchest
> Busy labourers in the belly's service, to be drawn
> From out each slave's greased mouth, which soon,
> From incapacity, would lose the habit
> Of eating.

In the mirror of poetry the half-century flashes by. The same things happened in poetry as in fiction. There was first the poetry of individual sensibility, then the social poetry and in a strange way the chaos, and now we seem to be on the threshold of a synthesis, in which the individual, having undergone these storms, is putting forward a personal view again. Up to 1930 the reign of Eliot continued undisturbed. The impact in 1917 of *Prufrock* (written in 1911), of the poems of the 1920 volume, and *The Waste Land* in 1922, was reinforced by the *Hollow Men* in 1925, and *Ash Wednesday* in 1930. It is difficult to pin down in a few words just what Mr. Eliot has done. Speaking to himself, he has found himself speaking for thousands. The summit of his achievement at the moment is *Four Quartets*, a musical structure and a philosophical structure, rooted in the oldest of scientific explanations of the nature of the universe, the four elements of earth, air, fire and water. It is a poetry made out of many elements, but above all, as all poetry must be, out of words. When he speaks of this struggle Mr. Eliot perhaps tells us more than he thinks:

So here I am, in the middle way, having had twenty
    years—
Twenty years largely wasted, the years of *l'entre deux
    guerres*—
Trying to learn to use words, and every attempt
Is a wholly new start, and a different kind of failure
Because one has only learnt to get the better of words
For the thing one no longer has to say, or the way in
    which
One is no longer disposed to say it. And so each venture
Is a new beginning, a raid on the inarticulate
With shabby equipment always deteriorating
In the general mess of imprecision of feeling,

Undisciplined squads of emotion. And what there is to
    conquer
By strength and submission, has already been discovered
Once or twice, or several times, by men whom one
    cannot hope
To emulate—but there is no competition—
There is only the fight to recover what has been lost
And found and lost again and again:

It is the problem he has discussed in his finest piece of
criticism, *The Music of Poetry*. The turning point of his
work is perhaps in *The Hollow Men*, the last word of
farewell to an old world. It is all esoteric poetry which
has taken more than thirty years to communicate. It is
interesting in this connection to recall Rainer Maria
Rilke's comment on his own "Elegies" in December,
1923: "The nature of these poems, their condensation and
abbreviation, the fact that they frequently name lyrical
totals instead of enumerating the various steps necessary
to reach the result, seems to intend them to be grasped
generally by the intuition of a person with similar
tendencies, rather than by what is called the understanding." In 1930, with *Ash Wednesday*, Mr. Eliot seemed to
many of his admirers to have taken a path along which
they could not follow him, the path of religion, but
nobody could have predicted that his successor and for
a while his supplanter would be Mr. W. H. Auden,
any more than anyone could have predicted that Mr.
Auden's successor would be the neo-romantic Mr. Dylan
Thomas.

In 1930 Mr. Auden's volume of *Poems* showed the

other path, the path of politics, signposted with a new idiom—the idiom of social awareness and of the complex mechanism of up-to-date civilization, an idiom which had an uncanny power of getting under the reader's skin:

> Watch any day his nonchalant pauses, see
> His dextrous handling of a wrap as he
> Steps after into cars, the beggar's envy.
> "There is a free one" many say, but err.

Or elsewhere:

> the intolerable neural itch,
> The exhaustion of weaning, the liar's quinsy,
> And the distortions of ingrown virginity.

In Auden and Spender and Day Lewis and MacNeice, it was a poetry of pylons and internal combustion engines, express trains, aeroplanes, frontiers, military manœuvres, decaying factories, arterial roads and rusting engines. It was full of social injustice, of economic depression and looming war. It was deliberately political. It existed in that uneasy gap between the great slump and the Second Great War. All these poets and their prose-writing companions were in the main socialists, and all were that sad and almost criminally careless thing, "premature anti-Fascists." The psychological situation was particularly interesting. They were, as they confessed frequently, men like Christopher Isherwood particularly, involved in a struggle against "the Father" as an authority from which an escape must be made, and against "the Mother" from whose entanglements and clutches it was equally necessary to emerge. The novels of Christopher Isherwood, and Auden and Isherwood's play *The Ascent of F.6* show this with very great clarity. The other psychological pattern is also seen clearly in the confessions of writers in or associated with the group. Mr. Isherwood wrote in 1934: "we young writers of the middle twenties were all suffering, more or less consciously, from a feeling of shame that we hadn't been old enough to take part in the European War." And George Orwell, looking back in 1940, said: "I am convinced that part of the reason for the fascination that the Spanish Civil War had for people of about my age was that it was so like the Great War." In Mr. Isherwood's autobiography, *Lions and Shadows*, and Mr. Cyril Connolly's *Enemies of Promise* we see the figures of that period.

Poetry was intimately bound up with this movement which many of its participants are trying to explain away, and from which they are trying shamefacedly to dissociate themselves. There is nothing shameful in having been young. The only shame is to spit on one's youth. However misguided this group may seem to have been, in the eyes of those wiser after the event, they all lived for their beliefs and some of them even died for them.

It is curious how many forms their foreboding of the coming war took, even humour. Mr. Auden is one of the wittiest of poets, and on the border of wit and schoolboy humour he lightens the grim seriousness of some of the group. This is how, in his *Journal of an Airman* he describes the "softening up" of an enemy country: "A preliminary bombardment by obscene telephone messages for not more than two hours destroys the morale already weakened by predictions of defeat made by wireless-controlled crows and card packs. Shock-troops equipped with wire-cutters, spanners and stink-bombs, penetrating the houses by infiltration, silence all alarm-clocks, screw down the bath-room taps, and remove plugs and paper from the lavatories."

The "softening up" of the reading public in England was not done by means of wireless-controlled crows or stink-bombs. It was done through periodicals and miscellany volumes. The first attack was in the volume *New Signatures* in 1932 and *New Country* in 1933, both edited by Michael Roberts, whose recent death has left a serious gap. It is Michael Roberts's selection of the poems and his Preface in *The Faber Book of Modern Verse* which has very largely governed poetical taste in England since 1936. Roberts put clearly the position of the younger social and political poet. "As he sees more and more clearly that his interests are bound up with those of the working class, so will his writing clear itself from the complexity and introspection, the doubt and cynicism of recent years." The activities of publishing houses like Faber and Faber, and the Hogarth Press, and of theatres like the Group Theatre and Unity Theatre, reflect the extremes of the movement. In 1936 the group possessed a regular organ, *New Writing*, which began in rather a grand way for a popular movement, but in 1940 it became really popular in *Penguin New Writing*, which has only now been compelled to suspend publication. It would be difficult to exaggerate the importance of these two publications. In *New Writing* almost every new talent of the 'thirties and 'forties was discovered or launched. In *Penguin New Writing* these private discoveries were presented to anybody who had sixpence or ninepence to spend, and in wartime even ninepence wasn't very much. These Penguin volumes went into the pockets of factory overalls and of battle-dresses, and into air-raid shelters. They could be thrown away when absorbed, or passed on, or assembled religiously on a tiny bookshelf, or some special poem or short story or piece of criticism cut out and kept. It was all *contemporary literature*, literature growing, English and foreign "Work in Progress," tackling the problems, not of yesterday, but of to-day. And what was particularly exciting, in a curious way, was the practice of giving potted biographies of the contributors, making them real people: "Anastatius Blenkinsop was born in Manchester in 1920, the son of a car-park attendant. He has been a schoolmaster, a bricklayer, a bookmaker's assistant and a circus clown. The short story in the present number is an extract from the trilogy he is now writing on the Rise and Fall of the Chemical Industry." I take up two numbers completely at random. There are good stories by Lionel Trilling, William Sansom, J. F. Powers, Eudora Welty and Mary Lavin. There are poems by Louis MacNeice, Terence Tiller and George Barker, and critical articles by André Gide, Walter Allen, Peter Brook, and by the Editor, John Lehmann.

In my first lecture the view I took was a glimpse into the future from 1900 onwards. From that viewpoint it was a dwindling perspective, in which the years from 1930 to 1950 appeared of steadily decreasing importance vanishing into a haze or mist at the end. To-day, in this concluding lecture, I am looking from the end of the half-century, and this same period becomes more and more actual as it rushes up to 1950, which is just beneath our eyes. Then it was a distant background, now it is a close-up, with everything in the foreground. It is a period which I think many people experienced vividly at the time, without necessarily observing the critical and historical processes involved, experienced it, but let it rush by unchecked, unmeasured, uncounted. It is a period I have very vividly in my mind, because for ten of its years, from 1929 to 1938, I followed it very closely. I had to, because I had to write an annual survey of the literature of each of those years. I don't pretend to be a tipster, but when I look back at some of the books I picked out for special attention, I am comforted to find that some of my endorsements have at least not been contradicted.

Perhaps the chief talent of those years, a talent which seems, so far as the novel is concerned, to have burnt itself out, is Mr. Christopher Isherwood. There is the strange personal promise of his earlier books, *All The Conspirators* and *The Memorial,* and the huge episodic novel he planned on pre-Hitler Berlin, *The Lost,* of which *Mr. Norris Changes Trains* and *Goodbye to Berlin* are the only surviving fragments. While most writers in those days were centred in Paris, the writers of this group of the 'thirties, Auden, Isherwood and Spender, lived in Germany and sought their inspiration in German literature, German poetry, German theatre and German cinema. Even to the casual reader the vivacity of Mr. Isherwood's Berlin is overwhelmingly convincing. It is in a way the triumph of that mood of "reportage" which formed so large a part of writing in that period, portraits of cities, *Journey to a War*. It was the super-journalistic portraiture of an age. Sometimes, as in Mr. Isherwood's novels or Mr. Graham Greene's brilliant travel books *Journey Without Maps* and *The Lawless Roads*, it became a new category of creative autobiography, very much indebted to the montage technique of the cinema. Even to the casual reader this Berlin is vivid enough, but to anyone who has lived, however short a time, in Berlin before 1933, the picture is almost painfully authentic. I remember reading Mr. Isherwood's story *The Laudauers* when it first appeared, and realized that I knew the man he depicted, had been in the room he described, and I am told that no German writer then or since has captured so accurately the atmosphere of the time. Mr. Isherwood is also one of our few humorous writers.

Another member of the group was Mr. Edward Upward, whose *Journey to the Border* in 1938 is one of the achievements of the period. It is the best of the English Kafka novels, although Mr. Isherwood swears that Mr. Upward had not read Kafka. If that is true, then it seems as if all the laws of literary history are contradicted. But the paradox is that in this age of rapid communications

it is not necessary to have read an author to be influenced
by him. It is almost a great book. The difference is that
where Kafka presents the universal problems of right and
wrong, Mr. Upward offers the local problem of Right
and Left.

When I look back on those years, I recall books which
forced themselves on my attention and which I have never
forgotten. There were Mr. Frank Tilsley's books, *I'd do
It Again* and *Devil Take the Hindmost*, genuine contemporary novels, tragic struggles, with a breathless tempo
at the end, not quite as aggressive as the American
"proletarian" novels, but fit to rank with Mr. James
Hanley's work of the same period. The two great
"proletarians" who emerged from America in those
years were Robert Cantwell, whose *Land of Plenty* in
1934 was, in my recollection at least, for I have not gone
back to it since, one of the best "collective" novels ever
written. It is the story of a timber factory, and though it
is teeming with individuals, it is the factory itself which
is the hero. And there was Albert Halper's novel *The
Chute*, 1938, about the delivery chute of a mail-order
house, another impressive and terrifying book. The
American "proletarian" novel of the 'thirties was the
corporate novel, in which the masses writhe, struggle,
resist, dream, drug, rise and sink. *The Chute* is probably
the greatest of them. It shows the subservience of the
underdog, the criss-cross of petty ambition and petty
jealousy, the fear of destitution in a world of dwindling
industrial security, the class struggle. It deals in betrayal
of trust, abandonment of promises, wanton lust, despair

and tragedy, and yet it has a thread of individual life and hope running through it which turns what might have been raucous propaganda into a work of beauty. It is not like the rather sentimental expressionist morality play which Ernst Toller produced in *Masses and Men*, but something akin to Charlie Chaplin's film *Modern Times*, which came out two years before *The Chute*.

It was in these years also that the two great American writers Ernest Hemingway and William Faulkner produced what seem to me their finest works, both rather neglected and underesteemed even by their admirers. Of William Faulkner the best, for me, is *Pylon* (1935), a better picture of the hysterical tempo of the age than any I know. And the other is Hemingway's *To Have and to Have Not* (1937), again a completely misunderstood and misjudged work. It is the one book of the American slump which, in my opinion, is both a great and a durable book.

It was in those years too that the strange talent of Miss Ivy Compton-Burnett was unfolding itself, with its diabolical sense of human relationships. She underlines the excruciating agony which comes from excessive awareness of relation. She has transferred to fiction some of the quality of Browning's poem "In a Spanish Cloister." No group of characters in fiction has succeeded so well in conveying with such intensity and precision the exacerbations of community life. But there is one book which stands apart, and stands deliberately apart, from this aggressive political or individual contemporaneity, in its way one of the greatest books of the

half-century—*The Root and the Flower*, by L. H. Myers
in 1935. It is not a book of the ivory tower, but it con-
tradicts deliberately the hectic preoccupations of the age.
It urges that character and personality demand as much
connoisseurship as do the arts. It attacks spiritual vul-
garity, which the author believed was the deep-seated
canker in the heart of our civilization, and sets against
the universally praised refinements of æsthetic sensibility
the rarer virtues of moral sensibility. It is in many ways
the wisest, the calmest, and the most beautiful book of
its time.

This has been a digression, but a necessary digression—
for poetry, though it must always transcend the events
of the time, cannot be understood apart from those
events, especially in our day. But there are always poets
who seem to be apart from the louder-voiced movements, who do not seem so much "engaged," as it is now
the fashion to say, but who nevertheless are not detached
from the process which feeds them at every taking in of
breath, and every utterance of a syllable. In the house of
poetry there are many mansions. Among the older men,
who have remained independent in their different and
their unrelenting ways, there are Walter De La Mare,
Robert Graves, Frank Kendon, Edmund Blunden, Herbert
Read, Andrew Young, Edwin Muir and L. Aaronson. In
the following generations the names of serious poets
abound, and I hope I am not doing an injustice to some
equally good, who have escaped my memory at the
moment. The serious ones are, among others, and on many
different levels, Dylan Thomas, Vernon Watkins, George

M

Barker, Lawrence Durrell, Terence Tiller, Roy Fuller, David Gascoyne, and among the women, Kathleen Raine and Anne Ridler. I am not passing judgment; I am merely expressing my gratitude to some of those who have given me pleasure, of different kinds and on different levels, in varying moods.

I wonder if I have made it clear how much serious modern literature has come to us from America, the other English-speaking world: the plays of Eugene O'Neill and Tennessee Williams, the novels of Hemingway, Dos Passos and William Faulkner, as well as those proletarian writers of whom I have just spoken. But I want to say firmly that some of the greatest living poets writing in English are Americans. I find that among these American poets I like best men like John Crowe Ransom and above all Wallace Stevens: they make me go all out, they exercise me, they stop me being lazy, they are taskmasters, they make me give all my faculties, even deceptively simple and straightforward poets like Robert Frost, and I am happy among the clowns—the Shakespearean clowns, I mean, like E. E. Cummings. It has been rather difficult in England to get hold of these poets and their interesting younger fellows, but there has just been published an anthology of *Modern American Poetry*, with critical and explanatory essays, edited by Mr. B. Rajan, an excellent opportunity of becoming acquainted with these varied and stimulating writers.

I have felt it necessary to dwell a little more closely than usual on the 'thirties because they and the 'twenties are the background of the young writers to-day. I remember that when I first began to be aware of literature as a thing separate from books, somewhere about 1912, it was the 'nineties—the 1890's—which had to be absorbed and departed from. Now it is the 'twenties and the 'thirties. But it is seldom that an epoch finds itself so sharply divided from the next, as this one was with the coming of war in 1939. Mr. Eliot, who is in no sense a political writer, put the situation perfectly in his *Idea of a Christian Society* in 1939. "I believe," he wrote very soberly and very quietly, "that there must be many persons who, like myself, were deeply shaken by the events of September, 1938, in a way from which one does not recover; persons to whom that month brought a profounder realization of a general plight. . . . The feeling which was new and unexpected was a feeling of humiliation, which seemed to demand an act of personal contrition, of humility, repentance and amendment; what had happened was something in which one was deeply implicated and responsible. It was not, I repeat, a criticism of the Government, but a doubt of the validity of a civilization."

I must now speak of the 1950's. What can we expect to happen? My guess is as good, or as bad, as the next man's. I think we are going to see some very exciting and wonderful things in the next ten years, even if there is another war. And, by the way, what does a war do? Quite apart from mobilizing writers and forcing them to face or evade fundamental problems, a war forces a writer into contact with types, idioms and accents not normally of his own circle, the living speech that reflects the living temperament, the fish queue, the markets, the barrack-room, three months in a cargo boat going round the Cape: the air-raid shelter, the officers' mess, the small back room. It settles down later, but that is the chief stimulant. The other side of the medal from this is the position of the exile. The exile from his own country fades out because he has lost the living envelope of speech in which he is wrapped daily, so that even though he is still using his own language, he is writing, as it were, in translation. Even Henry James shows signs of this.

The best play of the 1914–18 War was born of some such forced contact. The best play of that war is J. R. Ackerley's *The Prisoners of War* in 1925, not, certainly not *Journey's End*. I should like to see it revived, now that the art of stage production is a quarter of a century older, produced by Peter Brook, or Michael Benthall, or Michel St. Denis, or by all three in turn even. The best play born indirectly of war, is Bernard Shaw's best play *Heartbreak House*, which may ultimately come to be considered the chief English play of the half-century. I am glad that he also thought it his best play. But I wonder what he would have said had Mr. Ackerley called *his* play "Heartbreak House," as he might well have done.

And what about the future of the novel. There again I think the prospects are very bright. Every novelist seems concerned about "The Future of the Novel." Dozens of them have written about it, they really are concerned about it, and not merely about their own future. Henry Green, Walter Allen, Joyce Cary, C. P.

Snow, Philip Toynbee, V. S. Pritchett, Elizabeth Bowen, Graham Greene and Alex Comfort have all written about the novelist's problems, and I think we are beginning to see what is likely to happen. One encouraging sign is that they are all aware of a continuity in the novel itself, of the presence of the great masters, of what the great masters, older or more recent, have done for the novel, and can still do, and what they have done for the old masters. I suppose I must have read during the last six months more than a thousand serious reviews of novels and of the progress of fiction during the past ten years, and I have been struck by the seriousness with which the art of the novel and the problems of its future are taken, as much as I have been struck by the frivolity in another thousand reviews of what I can only call publishers' fodder. It was thirty-two years ago that Mr. Eliot, in his essay on "Tradition and the Individual Talent," wrote that "what happens when a new work of art is created is something that happens simultaneously to all the works of art which preceded it. The existing monuments form an ideal order among themselves, which is modified by the introduction of the new (the really new) work of art among them." The whole of literature since then, and most of all the novel, has shown the working of this process.

I have tried to show as exactly as possible, in these lectures, what is new in the literature of our century, and in some cases how old that newness is. The novelists are always on the look-out for this essential newness in older writers, applying any older formula, for which the age was not then ripe, to the immediate problems of to-day, and exploring further the methods which the original inventor did not himself fully exploit or which were "surplus to his requirements" of the moment. Some of them turn to the large reservoir of craftmanship which was Zola. Dostoevsky and Gogol and Tolstoy are still huge repositories of example, and James Joyce is an unworked and almost unexplored quarry. So long as the writer has something to say, he is grateful for any hint of a shape in which to deliver his message, or any tips in technique for the actual delivering of it. They say, as people used to say during the war, "We could let you have any amount of stuff, if we could only get the bottles." Many of the really great men of the past, it is true, have invented their own forms as well.

All these writers are agreed about one thing, the profound influence of the cinema on modern fiction, whether by giving the novelist a panoramic view from a height, or by forcing him to break his work up into tiny scenes, or by insisting on a narrative style in which not dialogue, which is the smallest part of a talkie, but carefully balanced fragments are united into a resultant impression, or in a score of ways for which we have not yet evolved a conscious label. It is not merely the daily commercial cinema, which has the same kind of effect as the newspaper or the novelette, but the serious films, from Russia, Germany, France and Italy, which we used to show at the Film Society or could be seen later at the Shaftesbury Avenue Pavilion or the Academy Cinema, and can be seen now in the whole network of film societies all over the country: *Dr. Caligari, Potemkin, The General Line, Storm over Asia, Earth, Warning Shadows, Le Million, Sous Les Toits de Paris, Citizen Kane,* and *Quai des Brumes.* These are as much part of the background of literature as the novels from abroad.

The reason why I feel so hopeful about the future is largely to be found in the essential humility of so many of the new writers. In poetic drama, which has a modest long-term policy, there have been humble beginnings and there should be large achievements. And this will be reflected in prose drama written by those who have not the poetic element in them, but who will be awakened because the roots of drama have been stirred up. In the novel the past five years have seen a large number of new novelists, of first novelists of surprising maturity and promise. Hardly a month passes by without something appearing which calls for serious attention. I think of Mr. Anthony West's *On a Dark Night*, of Mr. Chapman Mortimer's *The Stranger on the Stair*, of Mr. William Sansom's very sensitive book *The Body*, of Mr. P. H. Newby's novels, of volumes of short stories like Mr. Angus Wilson's *The Wrong Set* and *Such Darling Dodos*, and other books like Mr. J. D. Scott's crisp and assured novel *The Cellar*, which I was able to purchase for a shilling from the remainder shelf. It is indeed scandalous that this should happen. From America there is Mr. Irwin Shaw and Mr. Delmore Schwartz, and perhaps, Mr. Truman Capote and Mr. J. Horne Burns.

The best book of the recent war, and a work of art in its own right was, I think, Mr. Henry Green's novel

Caught, which immortalized the world of the fire services, as Mr. Henry Moore's air-raid shelter drawings have fixed for ever the face of another aspect of the air-raids. *Caught* arises from that special condition of war which I have already discussed, the forcible contacts established between inhabitants of completely separate worlds. Mr. Green is not one of the new novelists—he goes back, in fact, to 1926—but each of his novels faces a new problem, as Virginia Woolf's did in her time and Miss Compton-Burnett's do now. *Caught* deals in one way with the problem of loneliness, which is one of the problems to-day in peace, and even more so in war. Nothing fixes that terrible situation more firmly in my mind than an experience I had in Bristol during the war. I was waiting for a bus, and there came to the bus-stop two women, both evacuees from London, who were slightly acquainted. One asked the other how she liked living in the houses on the hill, and her reply was a summary of the horrors of modern city life: "Quite nice—more like friends than neighbours!"

It is this terrible loneliness which is the writer's problem, as it is the problem of any artist. It appears in Romain Rolland's fine book on Michelangelo. "I am always alone, and I speak to no one," wrote Michelangelo to his nephew. Loneliness and the dispersal of energies. Michelangelo refused an invitation to a party because, he wrote, "You are all so highly gifted that if I accepted your invitation I should lose my liberty. Each of you would steal a portion of myself. Instead of being rested, fortified, calmed by your society, my soul would be torn and dispersed to every wind that blows, so much so that for many days afterwards I should not know in what world I was moving." The self-centred artist—and all artists must be self-centred—must steel himself against these demands on his imagination, even though he cannot exist without them, but he must have sympathy, he must have encouragement, he must have understanding. He must have some kind of solidarity.

I have omitted to speak of the novels of André Malraux, because he would have taken me too far from my path, but now that I have spoken of the 'thirties, I must say a word about him in passing. He is, with Ignazio Silone, perhaps the greatest product of that special predicament of the 'thirties, the problem of solidarity, whatever he has become since then. In his book *La Condition Humaine*, (*Man's Estate*), translated originally under the foolish title of *Storm over Shanghai*, and in *Days of Hope*, he presents the eternal problem of the maintenance of human dignity and of man's desire to establish solidarity with his fellows in such a way as to preserve that dignity. The contemporary setting of war in China and war in Spain makes the problem even less local and even more universal. But the young writer still has his personal problem, which is no less agonizing now than it was when Joseph Conrad wrote to James Huneker in 1909: "When you overwhelm me with the mantle of Flaubert, it is an ominous garment to put on a man's shoulders. Yet there is one point in which I resemble that great man; it is in the desperate heart-breaking toil and effort of the writing; the days of wrestling as with a dumb devil for every line of my creation."

I have called this lecture "The Verdict," but not because I am so presumptuous as to think I can offer a judgment. I have tried to let the facts speak for themselves, the familiar facts, with only such manipulation as befits an honest advocate convinced of his case. A verdict can be reached only after a summing up. In these lectures you have heard only the case for the defence. You have all your lives been hearing the case for the prosecution. Literature is always on trial, and it suffers from those pests among so-called critics, the common informer and the smearer, as well as the knowing one, the smart-aleck and the entertainer. The most maddening verdict to the artist is: "Not guilty, but don't do it again." No names, no pack drill! But since the name of Edmund Gosse has cropped up in Virginia Woolf and in Sir Osbert Sitwell's recent volume of *Noble Essences*, I cannot resist making an exception, and quoting Mr. Eliot's cry from the heart on behalf of serious literature: "I cannot conceive of a future society in which Sir Edmund Gosse would be possible; and there will be many other popular entertainers for whom there will be no demand."

It is a sad thing that among the enemies of literature there are so many people who imagine themselves lovers of literature, and are lovers of literature, but who will not permit literature to advance beyond the stage at which they themselves discovered it. Their own modernity remains the frontier line. On the other side of the iron curtain, as on the old maps, there stands the

inscription, "Here are monsters, here are dragons." They
are the people who cry that they know what they like,
when all the time they only like what they know.

There must be no hardening of the arteries, no following of the safe line, no placid lapsing into the academic.
If there is to be a renaissance—and there are already signs
that there will be—there must be experiment. Without
experiment literature is dead, without experiment the
age is dead. But it must be honest experiment, not smart-
ness, not catch-penny cleverness, not snobbishness, but
grim, independent, even verbal experiment, with a
constant reassessment in the light of literary history, with
a climate of opinion to support it and a critical magazine
to encourage it. It is necessary to know what is going on,
and what has been going on in the past. It works both
ways. I remember Mr. Edgell Rickword once writing
that "if it had not been so frequently assumed that a
critic who cannot deal intelligently with a contemporary
becomes, by some queer metamorphosis, intelligent when
discussing a classic, literary history would not have become
the dust-bin that it is."

A climate of opinion to support the progress of literature, and a critical magazine to encourage it! *The Criterion*
is dead. *Horizon* is dead, *New Writing* is dead. In America,
the only place where criticism is still consistently main-
tained at the highest possible level, there are at least four
important critical reviews. *The Kenyon Review, The
Sewanee Review, Partisan Review* and *The Hudson Review*.
In England we have only *Scrutiny*. The problem is quite
simple. The *Edinburgh Review*, a hundred and fifty years

ago, was founded "in order to accustom English country gentlemen to the reading of printed books." The "New Criticism" in England and America set out more recently and more modestly to teach Professors of English literature how to ready poetry. The profoundest need of the moment in literature is for a new literary periodical whose function it will be to blow away the false and to maintain standards, and to keep the writer and the reader in touch with the best that is being done everywhere, in England, and North and South America, in France and Germany and Italy and Spain and Scandinavia, and in Russia and the East. This must not be a coterie review, nor must it be dogmatic and esoteric. The coterie review is a kind of family to feel warm in. *The Criterion* was a kind of church to feel confidence in. The periodical we now need must be catholic and ruthless, it must be independent, it must be the organ of no group or body. Its function will be, not to sell books, but to make books worth buying. With such a periodical as his home, the young writer of the 1950's should no longer feel lonely.

A Selection of
TWENTIETH-CENTURY LITERATURE
published by
SECKER & WARBURG

ENGLISH

Norman Douglas	*South Wind*	7s.	6d.
J. E. Flecker	*Collected Poems*	6s.	
George Orwell	*Down and Out in Paris and London*	10s.	6d.
	Burmese Days	10s.	6d.
	Coming Up For Air	10s.	6d.
	Homage to Catalonia	10s.	6d.
	Animal Farm	6s.	
	Critical Essays	10s.	6d.
	Nineteen Eighty-four	12s.	6d.
	Shooting an Elephant	11s.	6d.
W. R. Rodgers	*Europa and the Bull*	10s.	6d.
Frank Tilsey	*I'd do It Again* (Guild Edition)	1s.	6d.
Angus Wilson	*The Wrong Set*	9s.	6d.
	Such Darling Dodos	9s.	6d.
	Hemlock and After	12s.	6d.

AMERICAN

John Horne Burns	*The Gallery*	15s.	
	Lucifer With a Book	12s.	6d.
Henry Miller	*The Air-conditioned Nightmare*	15s.	
Lewis Mumford	*The Culture of Cities*	21s.	
	The Condition of Man	25s.	
Lionel Trilling	*The Middle of the Journey*	12s.	6d.
	The Liberal Imagination	18s.	

FRENCH

Hervé Bazin	*Grasping the Viper*	8s.	6d.
Gabriel Chevallier	*Clochemerle*	10s.	6d.

Colette	Chéri and the Last of Chéri	12s.	6d.
	Creatures Great and Small	12s.	6d.
	Chance Acquaintances	12s.	6d.
André Gide	The Journals		
	Vol. I, 30s.; Vol. II, 30s.;		
	Vol. III, 30s.; Vol. IV, 35s.		
	Dostoevsky	10s.	6d.
	Strait is the Gate	9s.	6d.
	Fruits of the Earth	10s.	6d.
	Œdipus and Theseus	7s.	6d.
	If it Die	15s.	
	Corydon	9s.	6d.
Jules Supervielle	The Colonel's Children	8s.	6d.
	The Survivor	9s.	6d.

GERMAN

Hermann Hesse	Steppenwolf (new edition in preparation)		
Franz Kafka	The Castle	12s.	6d.
	The Trial	12s.	6d.
	America	12s.	6d.
	The Great Wall of China	10s.	6d.
	In the Penal Settlement	12s.	6d.
Thomas Mann	Buddenbrooks	15s.	
	The Magic Mountain	18s.	
	Lotte in Weimar	10s.	6d.
	The Holy Sinner	15s.	
	Stories of Three Decades	15s.	
	Essays of Three Decades	21s.	

ITALIAN

Giuseppe Berto	The Sky is Red	5s.	
	The Works of God	8s.	6d.
	The Brigand	9s.	6d.
Alberto Moravia	The Fancy Dress Party	4s.	6d.
	The Woman of Rome	15s.	
	Conjugal Love	8s.	6d.
	The Conformist	15s.	
	Two Adolescents	12.s	6d.
Dino Buzzatti	The Tartar Steppe	12s.	6d.

Date Due